TEACHER EDUCATION PROGRAM EVALUATION

GARLAND BIBLIOGRAPHIES IN
CONTEMPORARY EDUCATION
(VOL. 10)

GARLAND REFERENCE LIBRARY
OF SOCIAL SCIENCE
(VOL. 619)

THE GARLAND BIBLIOGRAPHIES IN CONTEMPORARY EDUCATION

Advisory Editor:
Joseph M. McCarthy

TEACHER EDUCATION PROGRAM EVALUATION
An Annotated Bibliography and Guide to Research

Jerry B. Ayers
Mary F. Berney

GARLAND PUBLISHING, INC. • NEW YORK & LONDON
1990

Library of Congress Cataloging-in-Publication Data

Ayers, Jerry B.
   Teacher education program evaluation: an annotated bibliography
and guide to research / Jerry B. Ayers, Mary F. Berney.
      p.   cm. — (Garland bibliographies in contemporary education;
v. 10) (Garland reference library of social science; v. 619)
   Includes bibliographical references.
   ISBN 0–8240–3537–2 (alk. paper)
   1. Teachers—Training of—United States—Evaluation—Bibliography.
I. Berney, Mary F. II. Title. III. Series. IV. Series: Garland
reference library of social science; v. 619.
Z5814.T3A97   1990
[LB1715]
370'.71'0973—dc20   90–31529
                                                              CIP

Printed on acid-free, 250-year-life paper
Manufactured in the United States of America

CONTENTS

ACKNOWLEDGMENTS

We thank Paula E. Lester for suggesting this outlet for publication and the editiorial staff of Garland Publishing for accepting the proposal and providing assistance in completing the book.

John Centra, Larry Rudner, William Rutherford, and Nancy Zimpher are among those who provided annotations for important references. Boolie Stephens patiently searched for and annotated documents for this book as well as an earlier one.

Credit, but not blame, for proofreading goes to Patricia A. Eaves, Janine McClure, Boolie Stephens, and Teresa A. Thompson.

Joni E. Johnson coordinated the production and did a superb typing job, as always.

Staff at the Tennessee Technological Library and Edward Garten of the University of Dayton were helpful and patient with our repeated requests for assistance in checking references.

INTRODUCTION

TEACHER EDUCATION PROGRAM EVALUATION

The summative evaluation of teacher education programs has always been of interest to educators and members of the general public. In recent years, however, interest in both summative and formative evaluation has grown. Formative evaluations occur during the operation of a program and summative evaluations occur after a program is completed (Worthen and Sanders, 1987). Revisions in accreditation standards by the National Council for Accreditation of Teacher Education (NCATE) and other national, state, and regional agencies and in the certification or licensure requirements for teachers have both prompted and been prompted by the growing interest in evaluating teacher education programs.

This bibliography is intended to be of help to anyone who is planning the evaluation and subsequent re-design of a teacher education program. It will also be useful to anyone who is attempting to meet the evaluation requirements of various national and regional accreditation agencies and/or obtain approval from relevant state agencies. It represents an attempt to review relevant literature from January 1, 1976 through March, 1989. The exceptions to this include classic or landmark documents published prior to 1976 and documents which are currently in press and which will be available when this bibliography is published. The starting point was dictated by the paucity of documents cited prior to that date. The bibliography does not include an assessment of the quality of any research which may be represented in the documents, nor does the inclusion of a document represent the editors' endorsement of any viewpoints, research, methods, and techniques of evaluation.

1. STRUCTURE OF THE BIBLIOGRAPHY

Topics Covered

The bibliography focuses on the evaluation of teacher education programs by addressing the separate components of such programs (e.g., students, the knowledge base, governance, and follow-up studies). The bibliography has been divided into seven major categories, two of which have been further sub-divided to facilitate ease of use. Each category is described and illustrated by example in Section 3 of this introduction. Additionally, each entry is listed in the author, title, and subject indices and the relevant entries are listed in an index which is keyed to the NCATE standards.

Topics Not Covered

In keeping with its central purpose, this bibliography does not include references to teacher effectiveness or teacher attitudes except where such appear in documents which address related topics.

Reports on follow-up studies and the evaluation of field experiences from Canadian institutions and British studies on interviewing as part of the admissions process and a report from Scandinavia on field experiences represent the only contributions from outside the United States which are included in this bibliography. These studies are included because the results are applicable in the United States and they reinforce information presented in other documents.

Materials which are not readily available to the average users of this bibliography are not included, nor are conference papers or printed conference proceedings which are not generally available through the ERIC system. Also omitted are technical reports which are available only through their authors' institutions. It is to be hoped that these few omissions are far outweighed by the larger numbers of accessible documents which are included.

Sources of References

Three major index systems were reviewed as the primary means of locating documents to be included in the bibliography. These are: *Dissertation Abstracts International* (DAI), *Resources in Education* (RIE) and *Current Index to Journals in Education* (CIJE). The latter two sources are part of the Educational Resources Information Center (ERIC) system. *Books in Print* was also searched to ensure a more complete bibliography. Additional sources include the advance notices from publishers about pertinent books and monographs, and current periodicals.

Types of Documents Included

This bibliography includes books about evaluation, specifically teacher education evaluation. It also includes research reports, such as technical reports; journal articles which detail procedures, analyses, and results; dissertations; reviews of research; and essays. Some of the reports are quite technical and others are written in less technical language. Some reports are addressed to funding agencies and certain topics are covered by multiple reports or documents. Every effort was made to ensure that no document was cited twice, but documents with similar or even identical titles do occasionally appear.

2. HISTORY OF RESEARCH ON TEACHER EDUCATION EVALUATION

As the authors of many primers on educational evaluation explain, there is evidence of formal evaluations having been conducted as early as 2000 B.C. by the Chinese. Educational evaluation in the United States may be said to have begun with Joseph Rice's 1897-1898 study of students' spelling performance (Madaus and others, 1983, p. 6).

In the early 1900s, Thorndike began advocating the systematic measurement of human change. "The testing movement was in full swing by 1918, with individual and group tests being developed for use in many educational and psychological decisions" (Worthen and Sanders, 1987, p. 13). From 1920 through 1965 the testing movement continued to grow, with Smith and Tyler reporting the results of the Eight Year Study in 1942. The National Assessment of Educational Progress (NAEP) was "conceptualized by Tyler in the 1960s, following the approach used in the Eight Year Study" (Worthen and Sanders, 1987, p. 15). Whereas the Eight Year Study focused on outcomes, the accreditation movement addresses resources and processes in schools. Accrediting agencies developed guidelines for use in the formative evaluation of schools. Using these guidelines, educators began to consider resources and facilities, the adequacy of program design and the qualifications of faculty, components which are addressed today by accrediting agencies. The accreditation or professional judgement approach to evaluation can be traced to the establishment of the North Central Association of Colleges and Secondary Schools in the late 1800s, according to Madaus and others (1983). The movement did not gain widespread acceptance until the 1930s, when six regional accrediting associations were established across the United States. "Since then the accrediting movement has expanded tremendously and gained . . . credibility as a major means of evaluating the adequacy of educational institutions" (Madaus and others, p. 6, 1983).

The Elementary and Secondary Education Act (ESEA) of 1965 signified a new awareness of accountability. Project evaluations, to be conducted in accordance with specific guidelines and standards, were required. Rigorous training and dissemination programs in evaluation techniques were developed when it became apparent that it was not possible to meet the evaluation standards specified in the Act using existing instruments and evaluation techniques. One training and dissemination project, the Educational Training Consortium, was funded from 1972—1982. Brinkerhoff and others (1983) generated case studies based on actual situations for using evaluation to refocus a curriculum and for revising a curriculum to meet new certification requirements. The National Institute of Education (NIE) was established in 1972 and one of its research programs focused on educational evaluation. These are but two examples of the burgeoning recognition of evaluation as a means of improving education. Others are contained in the documents cited in this bibliography.

Educational evaluation is sometimes perceived of simply in terms of evaluating the effectiveness of teaching and there is an abundance of published works about evaluating the effectiveness of teachers. It seems, in fact, that each day's mail brings yet another brochure describing still another book or program for evaluating teachers and, as with any subject, the quality of these offerings varies greatly. There is, however, more to educational evaluation than evaluating instruction or its effectiveness. Teacher effectiveness is such a broad and controversial topic that it should have its own bibliography. It is not covered in this bibliography except tangentially under Faculty Evaluation.

An educational program, whether it is a university-based teacher preparation program or the elementary reading program in a school district, is comprised of and dependent upon many elements in addition to teachers. These elements include the physical plant, the library, the governance structure, and the students themselves—in short, the elements which are addressed in this bibliography.

3. OVERVIEW OF BIBLIOGRAPHIC TOPICS

The entries in this bibliography have been divided into categories, and in some instances, sub-categories. These are: (I) General Evaluation and Policy Analysis, (II) Knowledge Base and Quality Controls, (III) Students, (IV) Management and Governance, (V) Resources, (VI) Follow-up Evaluation, and (VII) Use of Information Utilization.

The category Students (III) is divided into four sub-categories: (1) Admissions; (2) Assessment of Progress; (3) Field and Laboratory Experiences, Student Teaching, and Internships; and (4) Outcomes Assessment. Sub-categories Faculty, Facilities, and Finances are included under Resources (V). Each category and sub-category is discussed in this section.

The editors attempted to categorize documents according to their primary emphasis, but where multiple topics are addressed in a single document, that document has been placed in the category that it addresses first or primarily. The subject index can be used to cross-reference topics.

I. General Evaluation and Policy Analysis

"General evaluation" is, as the label suggests, general and/or wide-ranging. Most of the references to policy analysis in teacher education in this bibliography are general in nature; linking the two is appropriate.

Abramson and Wholey (1981) are among the many authors cited who describe the organization and management of teacher education program evaluations. Ayers (1986) describes the development and subsequent implementation of a teacher education evaluation model over twelve years.

Evaluation models are discussed and described for circumstances ranging from comprehensive or generic (Greene and others, 1987; Cruickshank, 1984; Gephart and Ayers, 1988; Benz and Newman, 1986; Ayers and Berney, 1989) to specific (Ayers, 1980).

Borich (1974), Boruch and others (1981), Madaus and others (1983), and Herman, Morris and Fitz-Gibbon (1987) are the authors or editors of texts on evaluation models and approaches. Stufflebeam and others (1985) present a practical guide to conducting educational needs assessments.

Educational reform and accreditation is described by Gollnick and Kunkel (1986) and Howey and Gardner (1983). Research on teacher education is summarized and discussed in overviews by Lanier and Little (1986), Lasley (1986), and Sears (1988).

II. Knowledge Base and Quality Controls

In the revised NCATE standards (1987), "Knowledge Bases for
Professional Education" is the first category. Standard I. A. reads as
follows: "the unit ensures that its professional education programs are based
on *essential knowledge, established and current research findings, and sound
professional practice"* [emphasis added]. Much of what is written about
the knowledge base addresses one of those three areas.

Daiber (1979), Defino and Carter (1982), Johnston (1988), and
Jones (1988) discuss the need to develop and evaluate knowledge bases.
Clemens (1976) describes systems for maintaining and improving the
knowledge base of teacher education. Gideonse (1989) explains the 1987
NCATE standards relative to the knowledge base.

Quality controls make it possible to measure teacher education
programs against established standards. The program approval process
(Behling, 1984) is a quality control measure. Many documents cited in
this section describe practices in specific programs (Birch and Johnson,
1988 and Martonella, 1977) that are applicable to others. The current
reform movement will no doubt result in much more being published
about the knowledge base and quality controls in teacher education in the
near future.

III. Students

Admission policies; assessment of general progress; field and
laboratory experiences, student teaching, internships; and outcomes
assessment are covered in this section.

Admission. Applegate (1987) reviews four basic issues relative
to candidate selection. These four are purpose, standards, professional
judgment and legal and ethical considerations. Brubaker (1976) describes
a model for selection and retention in teacher education. Increasing
interest in evaluating candidates who wish to be admitted to teacher
education programs has led some states and institutions to require
admissions interviews. With the increasing emphasis on interviews,
research reports and discussions of the process will appear in the
literature, but at this time very little has been published on the topic.
One exception is Theodossin's (1983) study. Another area of concern is
the use of standardized tests such as the Pre-Professional Skills Tests
(PPST) and the National Teacher Examinations (NTE) as predictors of
successful teaching. A number of studies describe the relationships
between and among the standardized tests (Aksamit and others, 1987;
Heard and Ayers, 1988; Stoker and Tarrab, 1984). Studies that compare

education majors with students in other majors on such variables as entrance and exit test scores and grade point averages are included. The Cooperative Institutional Research Program's annual freshman surveys date from 1966 (Astin, 1985) and provide a wealth of information about potential teacher education majors. Comparisons of teacher education majors' entrance scores and other characteristics and their performance in student teaching are described by Ashburn and Fisher (1984). References to state-mandated testing are made by Anderson and others (1986). Barbe and others (1984); Barnes and Tierney (1983); and Marshman (1981) describe other testing concerns.

Assessment of general progress. This category addresses the routine evaluations which occur in individual courses—the assessment of student progress through paper and pencil tests, oral examinations, class presentations, portfolios, and other measures. Reighart and Loadman (1984) analyze students' reports of critical/significant events in introductory teacher education courses. Stuck (1984) examines cognitive and psychological development of students in an entry-level teacher education course. Boser and others (1986) compare students in traditional and alternative teacher education programs.

A number of researchers have looked at the evaluation of all phases of teacher education programs (Ashburn, 1984 and McNergney and Aylesworth, 1983). Stiggins (1984) investigates ways of improving assessment at all levels and Kozloff (1987) discusses ways of using assessment to promote development and enhance learning.

Field experiences, laboratory experiences, student teaching, internships. This category contains the largest number of documents in the bibliography, some of which must be considered primarily for their historical value. Student teachers' evaluations of their teaching experiences, preparation for student teaching, and supervising and cooperating teachers (Gallaher and others, 1983) are among the topics referenced in this section of the bibliography. Griffin and Edwards (1982) examine a variety of issues related to all aspects of student teaching, laboratory experiences, and evaluation. Cox and others (1981) and Silvernail (1980) describe two of many experimental programs cited in this bibliography that compare alternative approaches to the typical student teaching experience where one student teacher works with one cooperating and one supervising teacher. Zeichner (1983) describes some alternative approaches to conducting laboratory experience programs and Zimpher (1987) summarizes research studies relative to the role of the university supervisor in student teaching.

Outcomes assessment. Also referred to as "performance assessment," this is the summative evaluation of a student's years in a teacher preparation program. Many states require students to achieve a certain score on one or more components of the NTE. Some of the research reported in this bibliography is included for its historical interest; some is more current. Ayers (1988), Banks (1983), and Lovelace and Martin (1984) address the predictive validity of the NTE relative to teaching success. Cross (1985) discusses the NTE for use in decision-making relative to licensure. Rudner and Eissenberg (1988) look at the NTE as a licensure requirement and also a requirement for graduation. Ewell (1987), Moore and Markham (1983), and Scriven (1988) describe outcomes assessment programs. A lone voice (Ansah, 1985) asks, "Is testing necessary?"

IV. Management and Governance

Defining and establishing a system of governance within the college or university and the school, college, or department of education itself is one of the most critical aspects of a teacher education program. Roth (1983) explores the need to develop adequate systems of governance in teacher education programs. Orlosky (1988) analyzes the governance structure of teacher education programs and recommends procedures for preparing teachers.

Hearn demonstrates ways in which the governance structure at the university level influences the governance of the teacher education program (Ayers and Berney, 1989). Berneman (1977) and Khullar and Antonelli (1983) describe perceptions and attitudes of educators toward governance. Saphier and others (1989) discuss the role of decision-making in changing the governance structure of schools as classroom teachers become more proactive. This signals a trend which merits further investigation.

V. Resources

This category contains references to documents on the evaluation of faculty, finances, and physical facilities.

Faculty. Faculty members can be evaluated in terms of teaching, research or scholarly activities, and community or public service. The relative weight assigned to each area varies across disciplines and institutions. Much research and many descriptive reports focus on the evaluation of teaching; therefore, documents which address teaching comprise the greater part of this section.

Student rating instruments, faculty self-evaluations, and peer evaluations are described by Centra in Ayers and Berney (1989). Centra also discusses the evaluation of research and service; two areas which can be difficult to evaluate. Boyer (1987) suggests that the authoring of a text in one's field of expertise or authoring a reaction to a recent development in the field could be included in measures of scholarly activity.

The Joint Committee on Standards for Educational Evaluation published *The Personnel Evaluation Standards* in 1988. The Committee concurs with Miller's (1987) description of public service as "applied research, consultation and technical assistance, instruction, products, and clinical work on performance" (p. 66).

Physical facilities. This section contains references to the evaluation of libraries, laboratories, media centers, and other physical resources and facilities which support a teacher education program. The American Council of Research Librarians (ACRL) is one of the primary sources of information about libraries. Suggestions and guidelines, often including floorplans and wiring diagrams, for educational computing facilities are found in the many texts on the topic. Those are not referenced in this bibliography but are readily available in college libraries and bookstores, particularly where computer literacy is required of teacher education program graduates.

It is important that faculty be involved in planning any new facilities or any renovations of existing facilities to ensure a good fit between the facility and the teaching and learning activities it is intended to support. Foldsey (1985) and Glass (1984) are among the authors of documents included in this bibliography which address this issue. The Association of Physical Plant Administrators of Universities and Colleges (1985) provides details relative to evaluating higher education facilities. The Council of Educational Facilities Planners (1985) present space planning guidelines. Two additional sources of information about resources in higher education are the Association of Institutional Researchers (AIR), located at Florida State University, and the Society of College and University Planners (SCUP), located at the University of Michigan. Both of these organizations are international in scope and both publish frequent electronic mail newsletters which allow users to tap a vast network of colleagues.

Financial analysis. *New Directions in Institutional Research*, published by Jossey-Bass, is an excellent resource for financial and facilities planners. Hines and McCarthy's (1984) annotated bibliography of references to higher education finance should be useful in evaluating teacher education programs. Singly and together, Peseau and Orr address the myriad issues of funding teacher education programs (1979, 1980, 1982, and 1984); Manning and Swick (1984) also addressed funding in teacher education programs. Other documents in this section which are less directly related to teacher education programs are useful resources on policy analysis and other matters of planning.

VI. Follow-up Evaluation

Follow-up evaluations are probably the most widely used means by which personnel in teacher education programs learn how their graduates perceive the course of study and how the graduates' performance is perceived by principals, parents, supervisors, and others outside the institution. In fact, to be eligible for NCATE accreditation, institutions of higher education must meet ten Preconditions. Precondition 4 is directly related to follow-up evaluation and states:
"The unit keeps abreast of emerging techniques and regularly monitors and evaluates, both internally and externally, its operation, scope, quality of its offerings, and effectiveness of its graduates" (NCATE, 1987, p. 25).

As with all evaluations, follow-up instruments must be well-constructed. Craig writes that studies must be planned and conducted along sound lines and, most importantly, the results must be used to inform program improvement (Ayers and Berney, 1989). Adams (1987), along with a number of others in separate documents, discusses recent work in follow-up studies. Ayers (1989) summarizes follow-up study results over fifteen years in one example of the in-house studies which are included in this section of the bibliography.

VII. Information Utilization

The use of evaluation information is critical to the success of any effort to improve education, or any other endeavor. The collection of data in the absence of a plan for using it, and a plan for implementing the use, is a waste of resources. Findings about innovation and change are as applicable to education as to business and industry. The references found in this section of the bibliography address all aspects of a teacher education program. Hord and others (1987) provide a practical guide to organizing for and guiding change. Cross (1986) suggests that formative rather than summative evaluation is central to improving teacher education programs. It should be remembered that formative evaluation provides feedback for making revisions, whereas summative evaluation is a judgment about the worth of the object under consideration (Borich, 1974). Patton's (1986) book on utilizing evaluations for development and policy analysis is also referenced in this section. In one of several similar reports, Ryan (1985) describes the impact of evaluation data on those who are evaluated.

4. FUTURE DIRECTIONS FOR RESEARCH

The Road goes ever on and on
Down from the door where it began.
Now far ahead the Road has gone,
And I must follow, if I can,
Pursuing it with eager feet . . .

Tolkien, 1965, p. 62, 110

Educators, like Bilbo and Frodo, are on a Road which is not going to wait for us. We must keep moving, investigating new ideas, observing ideas in practice, reading journals to learn what colleagues can teach us, and contributing to the body of research and reports of good practice so that others may benefit from our successes. Evaluation and assessment issues are once again being labeled "important concerns" in education and that is good.

One example of the increased interest in evaluating programs is that the Fund for Improvement of Postsecondary Education (FIPSE), which is "the major funding source for assessment projects" has shifted its emphasis gradually from "assessment of individual students to the assessment of programs" (Cook, 1989, pp. 1-2).

John Goodland, president of The American Association of Colleges for Teacher Education (AACTE), "worries about education's being taken out of the hands of educators" (Monaghan, 1989, p. A3) and suggests that if educators can be heard over politicians, the necessary educational reforms could proceed more effectively. The nation's governors met during the summer of 1989 to discuss education but despite earlier statements about what some would like to see accomplished, did not set specific goals for higher education. Iowa's Governor Blanstad is credited with reporting that "the governors had reached the consensus that aspiring teachers should major in subjects other than education while they are in college" (DeLoughry, 1989, p. A21). Elsewhere, DeLoughry reports that Robert Atwell, president of the American Council on Education, "said he was sorry that the summit had failed to recognize explicitly the nation's education system as a 'seamless web' that includes higher education" (p. A24). The April 1989 issue of *Educational Leadership* was devoted to assessment. The May issue of the *Phi Delta Kappan* featured a number of articles on assessment. *Assessment Update*, a new quarterly publication, was born during the past year. All of these facts indicate that while educators have begun taking hard looks at our practices, we are not alone in that activity. Legislators, governors, and governing board members are both peering over our shoulders and studying our practices from their perspectives.

One example of positive action on the part of higher education comes from the National Association of State Universities and Land Grant Colleges Council on Academic Affairs which released a "statement of principles on student outcomes assessment" in November 1988. Its authors note that the criticisms of higher education expressed during the past decade and the belief "held by many public and some education officials that colleges and universities should be held accountable and should also develop reliable means to improve the quality of education" (1988, no page number) were among the factors which led to the formulation of the statement of principles. They further cite the growing requirements for state-wide student outcomes assessment and the push from accrediting agencies for "outcomes data as part of their review" as prompts to the issuing of the statement. The statement is preceded by a succinct rationale and consists of five principles; the entire document is printed on two sides of a single piece of paper and is well worth obtaining.

To maintain control of education and educational practices, we must develop nationwide standards for evaluating educational programs from pre-school through graduate school. Such standards must be agreed upon by all involved parties. A single set of standards for each educational level, from pre-school through graduate school, is necessary to avoid over-testing students and over-taxing teachers, administrators, and budgets. Evaluations must be cost effective and timely. Further work is needed to ensure that the instruments by which adherence to the new standards is measured are not prohibitively expensive and do not require so much time that the information they yield is out-dated before it is released.

We must continue to be proactive on our behalf or risk losing our right to choose and to direct educational reforms from our vast knowledge of what works and what does not and our pool of able researchers and practitioners.

REFERENCES

Abramson, M., and J. Wholey. "Organization and Management of the Evaluation Function in a Multilevel Organization." *New Directions for Program Evaluation* 10 (1981): 31-48.

Adams, Ronald D. "Follow-up Studies of Teacher Education Graduates." In *Advances in Teacher Education, Volume 3*, eds. Martin Haberman and Julie M. Backus, 181-201. Norwood, NJ: Ablex Publishing Company, 1987.

Aksamit, Donna, and others. "Relationships Between PPST and ACT Scores and Their Implications for the Basic Skills Testing of Prospective Teachers." *Journal of Teacher Education* 38 no. 6 (November/December 1987): 48-52.

Anderson, Betty, and others. *The Impact of State Mandated Testing on Teacher Education in Florida.* 1986. ERIC, ED 270 418.

Ansah, S. L. *Quality Teachers: Is Testing the Answer?* 1985. ERIC, ED 265 211.

Applegate, Jane H. "Teacher Candidate Selection: An Overview." *Journal of Teacher Education* 38 no. 2 (March/April 1987): 2-6.

Ashburn, Elizabeth A., and Robert L. Fisher. *Methods of Assessing Teacher Education Students.* 1984. ERIC, ED 255 493.

Association of Physical Plant Administrators of Universities and Colleges. *Professionals Working Together.* 1985. ERIC, ED 264 775.

Astin, Alexander W., and others. *The American Freshman: Twenty Year Trends, 1966-1985.* 1987. ERIC, ED 279 279.

Ayers, Jerry B. "Another Look at the Concurrent and Predictive Validity of the National Teacher Examinations." *Journal of Educational Research* 81 no. 3 (January/February 1988): 133-137.

Ayers, Jerry B. *Teacher Education Program Evaluation: A Case Study Past and Future.* 1986. ERIC, ED 275 669.

Ayers, Jerry B. *Teacher Evaluation in Early Childhood Education: Application of A Model.* 1980. ERIC, ED 186 110.

Ayers, Jerry B., and Mary F. Berney, eds. *A Practical Guide to Teacher Education Evaluation.* Boston: Kluwer Academic Press, 1989.

Banks, Ivan Winslow. "The Beginning Teacher Evaluation Instrument and Its Relationship To The National Teacher Examinations." Ed.D. dissertation, University of Kentucky, 1983.

Barbe, Richard, and others. *A Statewide Teacher Education Needs Assessment.* 1984. ERIC, ED 246 042.

Barnes, Carol P., and Dennis B. Tierney. *California's Problems in Operationalizing the Quest for Quality in Teacher Education.* 1983. ERIC, ED 235 172.

Behling, Herman E. *Quality Control of Teacher Preparation Programs Through the Program Approval Process.* 1984. ERIC, ED 250 300.

Benz, Carolyn R., and Isadore Newman. *Qualitative-Quantitative Interactive Continuum: A Model and Application to Teacher Education Evaluation.* 1986. ERIC, ED 269 405.

Berneman, Louis Paul. "The Governance of Teacher Education: A Struggle For Responsibility and Control." Ed.D. dissertation, Columbia University Teachers College, 1977.

Birch, Derek W., and Craig F. Johnson. *Quality Control/Assurance in Post Secondary Education: An Outcomes Approach.* 1988. ERIC, ED 298 859.

Borich, Gary. *Evaluating Educational Programs and Products.* Englewood Cliffs, NJ: Educational Technology Publications, 1974.

Boruch, Robert F., and others, eds. *Reanalyzing Program Evaluations.* San Francisco: Jossey-Bass, 1981.

Boser, Judith A., and others. *A Comparison of Participants in Traditional and Alternative Teacher Preparation Programs.* 1986. ERIC, ED 278 648.

Boyer, Ernest L. *College: The Undergraduate Experience in America.* New York: Harper and Row, 1987.

Brinkerhoff, Robert O., and others. *Program Evaluation: A Practitioner's Guide for Trainers and Educators.* Boston: Kluwer-Nijhoff Publishing, 1983.

Brubaker, Harold A. "Selection and Retention in Teacher Education: A Model." *Teacher Educator* 12 no. 1 (1976): 17-25.

Clemens, Thomas D. *The Dissemination and Utilization of Research and Development in Education--Two Strategies.* 1976. ERIC, ED 117 859.

Cook, Constance E. "FIPSE's Role in Assessment: Past, Present, and Future." *Assessment Update* 1 (Summer 1989): 1-3.

Council of Educational Facility Planners. *Space Planning Guidelines.* 1985. ERIC, ED 298 611.

Cox, C. Benjamin, and others. *A Study of the Effects of Pairing Social Studies Student Teachers.* 1981. ERIC, ED 222 429.

Cross, K. Patricia. *Using Assessment to Improve Instruction.* 1986. ERIC, ED 284 896.

Cross, L. H. "Validation of the NTE Tests for Certification Decisions." *Educational Measurement* 4 (1985): 7-10.

Cruickshank, Donald R. "Toward a Model to Guide Inquiry in Preservice Teacher Education." *Journal of Teacher Education* 35 no. 6 (November/December 1984): 43-48.

Daiber, Robert A. "Technology Education and Its Contribution to General Education." *Journal of Epsilon Pi Tau* 5 no. 2 (Fall 1979): 40-43.

Defino, Maria E., and Heather Carter, eds. *Changing Teacher Practices.* 1982. ERIC, ED 223 582.

DeLoughry, Thomas J. "Higher Education Pushed to Background, but Not Ignored, at the Education Summit." *The Chronicle of Higher Education* 36 no. 5 (October 1989): A21.

Ewell, Peter T. "Establishing a Campus-Based Assessment Program." *New Directions for Higher Education* 15 no. 3 (Fall 1987): 9-24.

Foldsey, G. *A Paradigm for Teacher Involvement in the Development of Educational Specifications.* 1985. ERIC, ED 267 021.

Gallaher, Thomas H., and others. "A Three Role Group Clinical Supervision System for Student Teaching." *Journal of Teacher Education* 34 no. 2 (March/April 1983): 48-51.

Gephart, William J., and Jerry B. Ayers, eds. *Teacher Education Evaluation*. Kluwer Academic Publishers, 1988.

Gideonse, Hendrik D. "Blackwell's Commentaries, Engineering's Handbooks, and Merck's Manuals: What Would a Teacher's Equivalent Be?" *Educational Evaluation and Policy Analysis* 8 no. 3 (Fall 1986): 316-323.

Glass, T. E. "Educational Specifications: A Blueprint for the Future Program." *CEFP Journal* 24 no. 1 (1984): 4-13.

Gollnick, Donna M., and Richard C. Kunkel. "The Reform of National Accreditation." *Phi Delta Kappan* 68 no. 4 (December 1986): 310-314.

Greene, Myrna L., and others. *Evaluating the Effectiveness of Alberta's Teacher Education Programs in Preparing Classroom Teachers*. 1987. ERIC, ED 280 825.

Griffin, Gary A., and Sara Edwards, eds. *Student Teaching: Problems and Promising Practices*. 1982. ERIC, ED 223 571.

Heard, Sharon A., and Jerry B. Ayers. "Validity of the American College Test in Predicting Success on Pre-Professional Skills Test." *Educational and Psychological Measurement* 48 no. 2 (Spring 1988): 97-200.

Hines, Edward R., and John R. McCarthy. *Higher Education Finance*. New York: Garland Publishing, 1984.

Hord, Shirley M., and others. *Taking Charge of Change*. Alexandria, VA: Association of Supervision and Curriculum Development, 1987.

Howey, Kenneth R., and William E. Gardner. *The Education of Teachers: A Look Ahead*. New York: Longman Inc., 1983.

Johnston, John M. *The Knowledge Base for Teacher Induction*. 1988. ERIC, ED 291 722.

Jones, Donald W. "Assessing the Knowledge Base in Teacher Education: A Fundamental and Necessary Task." *Teacher Education Quarterly* 15 no. 2 (Spring 1988): 20-31.

Khullar, Gurdeep S., and George A. Antonelli. *Comparative Analysis of the Basics of Teacher Education and Training.* 1983. ERIC, ED 242 672.

Kozloff, Jessica. "A Student Centered Approach to Accountability and Assessment." *Journal of College Student Personnel* 28 no. 5 (September 1987): 419-424.

Lanier, Judith E., and Judith W. Little. "Research on Teacher Education." In Wittrock, Merlin C. (ed.). *Handbook of Research on Teaching,* 527-569. New York: Macmillan Publishing Co., 1986.

Lasley, Thomas J., ed. *The Dynamics of Change in Teacher Education.* Washington: American Association of Colleges for Teacher Education, 1986.

Lasley, Thomas J., ed. *Issues in Teacher Education.* Washington: American Association of Colleges for Teacher Education, 1986.

Lovelace, Terry, and Charles E. Martin. *The Revised National Teacher Examinations as a Predictor of Teachers' Performance in Public School Classrooms.* 1984. ERIC, ED 251 416.

Madaus, George F., and others. *Evaluation Models: Viewpoints on Educational and Human Services.* Boston: Kluwer-Nijhoff Publishing Co., 1983.

Manning, M. L., and Kevin L. Swick. "Revitalizing Teacher Education: Fiscal and Program Concerns." *Action in Teacher Education* 6 no. 3 (1984): 76-79.

Marshman, Larry R. *Teacher Education Program Admission--A Case Analysis.* 1981. ERIC, ED 210 249.

McNergney, Robert, and Martin Aylesworth. *Preservice Teacher Education Evaluation: An Overview.* 1983. ERIC, ED 236 167.

Miller, Richard I. *Evaluating Faculty for Promotion and Tenure.* San Francisco: Jossey-Bass, 1987.

Monaghan, Peter. "'Healing' the Fractured Movement for Education Reform." *The Chronicle of Higher Education* 35 no. 27 (March 1989): A3.

Morris, Lynn Lyons, and Carol Taylor Fitz-Gibbon. *Evaluator's Handbook*. In *Program Evaluation Kit*, ed. Joan L. Herman. Beverly Hills, CA: Sage Publications, 1987.

National Association of State Universities and Land-Grant Colleges. *Statement of Principles on Student Outcomes Assessment*. Washington: NASULGC, 1988.

Orlosky, Donald E., ed. *Society, Schools, and Teacher Preparation*. 1988. ERIC, ED 296 996.

Orr, P. G., and Bruce A. Peseau. "Formula Funding is Not the Problem in Teacher Education." *Peabody Journal of Education* 57 (1979): 61-71.

Patton, Michael Quinn. *Utilization-Focused Evaluation*. Newbury Park, CA: Sage Publications, 1986.

Peseau, Bruce A., and P. G. Orr. "The Outrageous Underfunding of Teacher Education." *Phi Delta Kappan* 62 no. 2 (October 1980): 100-102.

Peseau, Bruce A., "Developing an Adequate Resource Base for Teacher Education." *Journal of Teacher Education* 33 no. 4 (1982): 13-15.

Peseau, Bruce A. *Resources Allocated to Teacher Education in State Universities and Land-Grant Colleges*. 1984. ERIC, ED 250 297.

Reighart, Penelope A., and William E. Loadman. *Content Analysis of Student Criterical Events Reported in the Professional Introduction Courses*. 1984. ERIC, ED 248 202.

Roth, Robert A. *The Redesign of Teacher Education in the United States: External Strategies: Competency Testing and State Program Approval*. 1983. ERIC, ED 233 001.

Rudner, Lawrence M., and Thomas E. Eissenberg. *Standard Setting Practices for Teacher Tests*. 1988. ERIC, ED 293 865.

Ryan, Alan G. *How Case Study Evaluations are Received by Those Who Are Evaluated.* 1985. ERIC, ED 267 094.

Scriven, Michael. "Duty-Based Teacher Education." *Journal of Personnel Evaluation in Education* 1 no. 4 (1988): 319-334.

Sears, James T., and others. *Teacher Education Policies and Programs: Implementing Reform Proposals of the 1980's.* 1988. ERIC, ED 296 985.

Silvernail, David. *Assessing the Effectiveness of Preservice Field Experiences in Reducing Teacher Anxiety and Concern Levels.* 1980. ERIC, ED 191 828.

Stiggins, Richard J. *Evaluating Students by Classroom Observation: Watching Students Grow.* 1984. ERIC, ED 243 941.

Stoker, W. M., and Miguel Tarrab. *A Study of the Relationship of Pre-Professional Skills Tests and American College Tests.* 1984. ERIC, ED 252 496.

Stufflebeam, Daniel L. *Conducting Educational Needs Assessments.* Boston: Kluwer-Nijhoff Publishing Co., 1984.

Theodossin, Ernest. *Selection Through Interviewing: Entrance Procedures in Teacher Recruitment.* 1983. ERIC, ED 267 036.

Tolkein, J. R. R. *The Hobbit.* New York: Ballantine Books, 1978.

Worthen, Blaine R., and James R. Sanders. *Educational Evaluation: Alternative Approaches and Practical Guidelines.* New York: Longman, 1987.

Zeichner, Kenneth M. "Alternative Paradigms of Teacher Education." *Journal of Teacher Education* 31 no. 6 (May/June 1983): 3-9.

Zimpher, Nancy L. "Current Trends in Research on University Supervision of Student Teaching." In *Advances in Teacher Education, Volume 3*, eds. Martin Haberman and Julie M. Backus, 118-150. Norwood, NJ: Ablex Publishing Company, 1987.

Teacher Education
Program Evaluation

I. GENERAL EVALUATION AND POLICY ANALYSIS

1. Abramson, M., and J. Wholey. "Organization and Management of the Evaluation Function in a Multilevel Organization." *New Directions for Program Evaluation* 10 (1981): 31-48.

   Describes useful techniques for the organization and management of evaluations of teacher education programs.

2. American Association of Colleges for Teacher Education. *Educating a Profession: Competency Assessment.* 1983. ERIC, ED 231 832.

   Explores the need for a system of evaluation in teacher education programs that assesses specific competencies, employs multiple assessment methods, and provides for continuous monitoring of student progress.

3. American Association of Colleges for Teacher Education. *The Preparation of Education Professionals for Educating Exceptional Students: A Resource for Responding to the NCATE Special Education Standards.* 1982. ERIC, ED 223 555.

   Explores various issues designed to help institutions meet the NCATE standards related to preparing teachers to deal with exceptional learners.

4. Ayers, Jerry B. *Design Characteristics for Meaningful Program Evaluation.* 1986. ERIC, ED 274 650.

   Recommends ten generic characteristics that are essential for the meaningful evaluation of a teacher education program.

5. Ayers, Jerry B. *Evaluation of Programs for the Preparation of Teachers of Young Children.* 1987. ERIC, ED 285 649.

    Presents a model for the evaluation of programs for the preparation of teachers of young children.

6. Ayers, Jerry B. *Teacher Education Program Evaluation: A Case Study Past and Future.* 1986. ERIC, ED 275 669.

    Describes the development and evolution of a teacher education program evaluation model that was used for 12 years.

7. Ayers, Jerry B. *Teacher Evaluation in Early Childhood Education: Application of a Model.* 1980. ERIC, ED 186 110.

    Reviews the application of the Tennessee Technological University Teacher Evaluation Model to programs for the preparation of teachers in early childhood education.

8. Ayers, Jerry B., and Mary F. Berney, eds. *A Practical Guide to Teacher Education Evaluation.* Boston: Kluwer Academic Publishers, 1989.

    Presents a comprehensive system for the evaluation of all aspects of a teacher education program.

9. Ayers, Jerry B., and others. "The Accreditation Plus Model." *Journal of Personnel Evaluation in Education* 1 no. 4 (1988): 335-343.

    Reports the development of a model that can be used in the evaluation of teacher education programs.

10. Ayers, Jerry B., and others. *Institutional Needs and Teacher Education Program Evaluation.* 1987. ERIC, ED 289 859.

    Identifies the teacher education program evaluation needs of small private institutions, regional and state universities, and large multi-purpose institutions.

11. Bain, Greg. *Evaluating Teaching: Purposes, Methods, and Policies.* 1982. ERIC, ED 289 431.

    Describes the development of a guide to the evaluation and improvement of teacher education programs which has application at a variety of institutions.

12. Baktash, Mohammed Reza. "Evaluation of Experimental Teacher Education: An Application of a Perception-Based Model to Experimental Teacher Education." Ph.D. dissertation, Saint Louis University, 1980.

    Describes the evaluation of the experimental teacher education program at Saint Louis University and the development of an effective working model for evaluation of experimental teacher education programs.

13. Bell, D., and G. Steinmiller. *Procedures for Serving Accreditation of Teacher Education Programs in Arkansas.* 1987. ERIC, ED 282 828.

    Summarizes the procedures for the accreditation of teacher education programs in the State of Arkansas.

14. Benz, Carolyn R., and Isadore Newman. *Qualitative-Quantitative Interactive Continuum: A Model and Application to Teacher Education Evaluation.* 1986. ERIC, ED 269 405.

    Presents a model for qualitative and quantitative evaluation research useful in the evaluation of teacher education programs.

15. Bernhardt, Victoria L. *Evaluation Processes of Regional and National Education Accrediting Agencies: Implications for Redesigning an Evaluation Process in California.* 1984. ERIC, ED 248 271.

    Identifies overlaps and gaps in the accreditation/evaluation processes of four different accrediting bodies and makes recommendations for the redesign of the Commission on Teacher Credentialing in California.

16. Beza, Jacqueline Bowen. "School of Education Faculty
    Assessment of Educational Reform." Ph.D. dissertation, The
    University of North Carolina at Chapel Hill, 1984.

    Reports the results of a survey of teacher education faculty
    attitudes toward the North Carolina Quality Assurance Program.

17. Bloomsburg University. *Planning for Change in Teacher
    Education at Bloomsburg University. An Ongoing Comprehensive
    Evaluation.* 1984. ERIC, ED 248 208.

    Reports the evaluation, planning, and implementation processes
    for improving a teacher education program.

18. Borg, Walter R. "The Educational R & D Process: Some
    Insights." *Journal of Experimental Education* 55 no. 4 (Summer
    1987): 181-188.

    Identifies the problems and strategies related to the planning,
    development of a prototype, and evaluating educational programs
    and instructional materials in higher education.

19. Borich, Gary. *Evaluating Educational Programs and Products.*
    Englewood Cliffs, NJ: Educational Technology Publications,
    1974.

    Outlines techniques for evaluating education programs.

20. Boruch, Robert F., and others, eds. *Reanalyzing Program
    Evaluations.* San Francisco: Jossey-Bass, 1981.

    Describes methods and techniques for the evaluation of
    educational programs.

21. Bossing, Lewis. *Summer Faculty Leave Project Report, 1979.*
    1979. ERIC, ED 186 365.

    Presents the results of a survey of admission and educational
    practice and policy evaluation at selected teacher education
    institutions.

22. Brinkerhoff, Robert O., and others. *Program Evaluation: A Practitioner's Guide for Trainers and Educators.* Boston: Kluwer-Nijhoff Publishing, 1983.

    Provides guidelines, resources, and references for evaluating educational programs; includes case studies of various types of evaluation problems and a design manual with worksheets and examples.

23. Brunkhorst, Gene Roland. "The Development of a Multicomponent Evaluation Model for Undergraduate Teacher Education Programs." Ph.D. dissertation, Saint Louis University, 1988.

    Examines the use of a multicomponent evaluation model for providing a continuous and comprehensive evaluation system for a teacher education program.

24. Burger, Michael Lynn. "The Identification of Important Teaching Skills: Combining Philosophical and Psychological Principles, Research Findings, and Legal and Accreditation Standards." Ed.D. dissertation, The University of Nebraska - Lincoln, 1980.

    Identifies a valid set of teaching skills and compares the degree of importance of these skills perceived by educators in Nebraska and national experts in the field of teacher education.

25. Camp, William G., and others. *A Model for Evaluating the Sources of Professional Esteem for Vocational Teacher Education Programs.* 1987. ERIC, ED 281 856.

    Summarizes the results of the application of a model for evaluating agricultural teacher education programs.

26. Canty, June Marie. "An Analysis of Expectation/Delivery Differentials Across Various Modes of Teacher Preparation." Ed.D. dissertation, University of Washington, 1983.

    Surveys the relationship between the perceptions of real and ideal teacher education programs held by students in the programs at the University of Washington and Western Washington University.

27. Cardia, Joseph Victor. "An Episodic Case Study of a Competency Based Teacher Education Program." Ed.D. dissertation, Columbia University Teachers College, 1982.

    Looks at the development, implemention, and evaluation of the Competency Based Teacher Education Program of a Long Island College.

28. Carpenter, H. H., ed. *Nicholls Teacher Education Program Evaluation Project (NTEP). Evaluation Model.* 1984. ERIC, ED 263 044.

    Develops a broad-based heuristic model for assessing both the products and processes of a teacher education program.

29. Carter, Judy Carolyn Luckey. "An Analysis of the University of South Carolina at Aiken Teacher Education Curriculum in Relationship to the Criteria Identified in the Georgia Teacher Education Model." Ed.D. dissertation, University of South Carolina, 1981.

    Analyzes the methods of evaluating student teachers at the University of South Carolina at Aiken and compares these methods with the Georgia Model for the development of a revised teacher education program.

30. Chelimsky, Eleanor. "The Politics of Program Evaluation." *New Directions for Program Evaluation* 34 (Summer 1987): 5-21.

    Looks at a five-part continuum evaluation process for the development of policy questions and their translation into knowledge that is credible, timely, responsive, and usable.

31. Chelimsky, Eleanor. *What Have We Learned About the Politics of Program Evaluation?* 1986. ERIC, ED 280 853.

    Discusses the politics of program evaluations and suggests ways to make evaluations credible, timely, and useful.

32. Clark, Mary Jo. "Academic Program Evaluation." *New Directions for Institutional Research* 10 no. 1 (March 1983): 27-37.

    Includes a review of case studies in teacher education program evaluation.

33. Clarken, Rodney. *Evaluating Teacher Education Graduates and Programs.* 1983. ERIC, ED 230 510.

    Recounts some of the issues related to evaluation of teacher education programs that must be addressed in order for small independent liberal arts colleges to meet the standards of such agencies as the National Council for Accreditation of Teacher Education.

34. Cohn, Marilyn Rae. "The Interrelationship of Theory and Practice in Teacher Education: A Description and Analysis of the LITE Program." Ph.D. dissertation, Washington University, 1979.

    Provides a description and analysis of the LITE Program used for the preparation of elementary education students at Washington University.

35. Coley, Richard J., and Margaret E. Thorpe. *A Look at the MAT Model of Teacher Education and Its Graduates: Lessons for Today.* 1985. ERIC, ED 272 457.

    Describes a system for the evaluation of Master of Arts programs for the preparation of teachers.

36. Connecticut State Department of Education. *Standards and Procedures for Approval of Teacher Preparation Programs.* 1984. ERIC, ED 263 055.

    Reviews the standards for the approval of teacher education programs in the State of Connecticut and makes suggestions relative to program evaluation.

37. Cook, Constance E. "FIPSE's Role in Assessment: Past, Present, and Future." *Assessment Update* 1 (Summer 1989): 1-3.

Provides an overview of the Fund for the Improvement of Postsecondary Education (FIPSE) funding patterns from its inception in 1972 through the present, noting an increased emphasis on funding assessment projects.

38. Cooper, James H., and others. "Needed: Systematic Evaluation of Teacher Education Programs." *Action in Teacher Education* 2 no. 3 (Summer 1980): 17-23.

Looks at a model for the evaluation of teacher education programs and provides the basis for collaboration among institutions engaged in similar efforts.

39. Crossen, Frederick. *The Philosophy of Accreditation.* 1988. ERIC, ED 292 436.

Discusses a variety of issues related to all types of program accreditation, including the importance of adequate systems for the evaluation of programs within the regional associations.

40. Cruickshank, Donald R. "Toward a Model to Guide Inquiry in Preservice Teacher Education." *Journal of Teacher Education* 35 no. 6 (November/December 1984): 43-48.

Outlines an inquiry model for teacher education programs and includes a scheme for evaluation.

41. Daugherty, Richard F. "An Evaluation of the Undergraduate Education Program of the University of Wyoming." Ed.D. dissertation, University of Wyoming, 1985.

Compares 1966 students' perceptions of their teacher education programs with the perceptions of 1981-83 students.

42. deVoss, Gary, and others. *A System for Documenting and Evaluating the Experiences of Pre/Inservice Teachers.* 1981. ERIC, ED 211 500.

   Uses the Student Information System as a means of receiving feedback and evaluating the teacher education programs at The Ohio State University.

43. Dickson, George E., and William Wiersma. *Empirical Measurement of Teacher Performance.* 1984. ERIC, ED 263 211.

   Investigates a continuing effort to evaluate a competency-based teacher education program.

44. Dickson, George E., and William Wiersma. *Measurement of Teacher Competence.* 1982. ERIC, ED 223 552.

   Explores a system for the evaluation of a competency-based teacher education program.

45. Dickson, George E., and William Wiersma. *Research and Evaluation in Teacher Education: A Concern for Competent, Effective Teachers.* Toledo, OH: The University of Toledo, 1980.

   Presents a summary of a comprehensive system for the evaluation of teacher education programs.

46. Dillon, J. T., and Stanley S. Starkman. "A 'Model' Approach to Evaluation of Teacher Education Programs." *Education* 101 no. 4 (Summer 1981): 366-371.

   Uses a six part model for the evaluation of teacher education programs.

47. Doak, J. Linward. *Regional Universities' Needs for Conducting Teacher Education Evaluation: A Case Study of Eastern Kentucky University.* 1987. ERIC, ED 290 766.

   Reports a case study of program evaluation at Eastern Kentucky University.

48. Dravland, Vern, and Myrna Greene. *Development of a Model for the Evaluation of Teacher Education Programs.* 1979. ERIC, ED 177 171.

     Outlines a qualitative analysis evaluation system for teacher education programs that is designed to follow students from admission into the university through the education program and their first five years of teaching in the schools.

49. Dressel, Paul, and Lou Anna Kimsey Simon. "Annual Review and Evaluation." *New Directions for Institutional Research* 11 (1976): 87-106.

     Presents a basic model for the continuous evaluation of academic departments at Michigan State University.

50. Eastern Kentucky University. *Eastern Kentucky University: A Comprehensive Teacher Education Program/Product Evaluation.* 1983. ERIC, ED 248 200.

     Describes a system for evaluating the teacher education programs at Eastern Kentucky University.

51. Everston, Carolyn, and others. *The Characteristics of Effective Teacher Preparation Programs.* 1984. ERIC, ED 250 314.

     Examines the characteristics of effective teacher education programs and describes ways of conducting evaluations.

52. Ewell, Peter T. *Recruitment, Retention and Student Flow: A Comprehensive Approach to Enrollment Management Research.* Boulder, CO: National Center for Higher Education Management Systems, 1985.

     Offers a comprehensive management plan for recruitment, retention and student flow in higher education.

53. Ewell, Peter, T., and Robert P. Lisensky. *Assessing Institutional Effectiveness.* Boulder, CO: Consortium for the Advancement of Private Higher Education, 1988.

     Outlines ways of measuring institutional effectiveness in achieving goals.

54. Falcone, Nina Fernando. "Evaluating The Products of a Teacher Education Program." Ed.D. dissertation, Columbia University Teachers College, 1978.

    Describes an examination of the secondary English teacher education program at Jersey City State College by examining data on outcomes of graduates and characteristics of the teaching performance of graduates.

55. Fetterman, Mary Anne Pitman, ed. *Educational Evaluation: Ethnography in Theory, Practice, and Politics.* Beverly Hills, CA: Sage Publications, 1986.

    Outlines the use of ethnographic analysis in the evaluation of educational programs.

56. Floden, Robert E. "Flexner, Accreditation, and Evaluation." *Educational Evaluation and Policy Analysis* 2 no. 2 (March/April 1980): 35-46.

    Provides a rationale and basis for the use of alternative approaches to the evaluation of teacher education programs.

57. Freeman, Donald. *Overview: Program Evaluation in the College of Education at Michigan State University.* 1986. ERIC, ED 281 830.

    Presents a model for the evaluation of undergraduate and graduate teacher education programs.

58. Freeze, Chester R., and others. *Reform Policies, Procedures and Standards for the Approval of Teacher Education Programs in South Carolina.* 1987. ERIC, ED 278 653.

    Summarizes the policies, procedures, instruments, and standards for the evaluation of teacher education programs in South Carolina.

59. Galluzzo, Gary R. *An Evaluation of a Teacher Education Program.* 1983. ERIC, ED 229 373.

    Describes the application of the Context-Input-Process-Product (CIPP) evaluation model developed by Stufflebeam to the evaluation of a teacher education program.

60. Gatchell, Irene Smith. "An Assessment of the Undergraduate Elementary Education Program at Louisiana State University." Ed.D. dissertation, Louisiana State University, 1978.

    Describes an evaluation of the elementary education preparation program at Louisiana State University.

61. Georgia State Department of Education. *Criteria for Approving Teacher Education Programs in Georgia Institutions.* 1983. ERIC, ED 244 941.

    Discusses the standards that were developed in Georgia for the evaluation of teacher education programs, including criteria for school services personnel programs.

62. Gephart, William J., and Jerry B. Ayers, eds. *Teacher Education Evaluation.* Kluwer Academic Publishers, 1988.

    Outlines a six part model for the evaluation of teacher education programs, including practical examples of implementation of the various parts of the theoretical model.

63. Gibney, T., and others. *CBTE Past and Present: The Toledo Experience.* 1987. ERIC, ED 280 818.

    Describes the ongoing process of evaluation and assessment of the current CBTE program that is in operation at the University of Toledo.

64. Gollnick, Donna M., and Richard C. Kunkel. "The Reform of National Accreditation." *Phi Delta Kappan* 68 no. 4 (December 1986): 310-314.

    Examines various issues related to the reform of national accreditation.

65. Grabon, Chad Lee C., "Development and Formative Evaluation of Educational Products Using Data Base Management Systems in a College of Education." Ph.D. dissertation, Iowa State University, 1985.

    Describes uses of Data Base Management Systems technology in the improvement and/or assessment of potential teachers in a college of education.

66. Greene, Myrna. *Improving Teacher Education through Program Evaluation*. 1985. ERIC, ED 268 172.

    Summarizes an ongoing comprehensive model of program evaluation which has as its major goal the improvement of teacher education.

67. Greene, Myrna L., and others. *Evaluating the Effectiveness of Alberta's Teacher Education Programs in Preparing Classroom Teachers*. 1987. ERIC, ED 280 825.

    Outlines the implementation of an ongoing comprehensive model of teacher education program evaluation.

68. Guba, Egon G., and Yvonna S. Lincoln. *Effective Evaluation: Improving the Usefulness of Evaluation Results Through Responsive and Naturalistic Approaches*. San Francisco: Jossey-Bass, 1981.

    Discusses evaluation practices in general that are applicable to educational programs and outlines in detail methods and techniques for improving the usefulness of evaluation results.

69. Haegel, Mary Ann. "A Study of Ph.D. and Ed.D. Programs in Fourteen Graduate Schools of Arts and Sciences and Graduate Schools of Education: 1950-1984." Ph.D. dissertation, Boston College, 1986.

    Analyzes the changes in Ph.D. and Ed.D. programs and whether the programs were substantially different.

70. Hanmeng, Nom. "Characteristics of Undergraduate Teacher
    Education Programs in Selected Teacher Education Institutions in
    the United States." Ph.D. dissertation, University of Missouri -
    Columbia, 1981.

    Summarizes the characteristics of various types of teacher
    education programs in the United States.

71. Hodgkinson, Harold L., and others. *Improving and Assessing
    Performance: Evaluation in Higher Education.* Berkeley, CA:
    Center for Research and Development in Higher Education,
    University of California, 1975.

    Examines means for the assessment and evaluation of various
    types of programs in higher education.

72. Hord, Shirley M., and others. *Toward Usable Strategies for
    Teacher Education Program Evaluation.* 1982. ERIC, ED 229
    370.

    Includes papers by teacher education practitioners and evaluation
    experts on teacher education evaluation.

73. Hord, Shirley M., and Ronald D. Adams, eds. *Teacher Education
    Program Evaluation, 1981: Theory and Practice.* 1981. ERIC,
    ED 204 329.

    Examines the status, need for, and ways of conducting teacher
    education program evaluation.

74. Howey, Kenneth R., and William E. Gardner. *The Education of
    Teachers: A Look Ahead.* New York: Longman Inc., 1983.

    Studies a variety of evaluation techniques useful in improving
    teacher preparation programs.

75. Johnson-Slaughter, Ida Bernice. "The Impact of the Teacher Corps Program on Teacher Education and Certification Requirements: A Case Study." Ed.D. dissertation, Washington State University, 1984.

    Examines the impact of the WSU/Pasco project on teacher education and certification and also examines related organizational factors.

76. Joint Committee on Standards for Educational Evaluation. *Standards for Evaluations of Educational Programs, Projects, and Materials.* New York: McGraw Hill, 1981.

    Provides a set of standards for use in conducting evaluations of educational programs (including teacher education programs), projects, and materials.

77. Jones, Alan H., and Peter L. LoPresti. *External Assessment: A California Case Study in Innovative Program Evaluation.* 1982. ERIC, ED 226 439.

    Describes the teacher education program assessment project in the State of California.

78. Jones, Donald W., ed. *Preparing for NCATE: Criteria for Compliance—External Evaluation.* Chicago: North Central Association of Colleges and Schools, 1988.

    Outlines the steps needed for compliance with the standards of the National Council for Accreditation of Teacher Education.

79. Koppelman, K. L. "The Explication Model: An Anthropological Approach to Program Evaluation." *Educational Evaluation and Policy Analysis* 3 no. 1 (July/August 1979).

    Outlines the use of anthropological methods in the evaluation of teacher education programs.

80. Lanier, Judith E., and Judith W. Little. "Research on Teacher Education." In *Handbook of Research on Teaching*, edited by Merlin C. Wittrock, 527-569. New York: Macmillan Publishing Co., 1986.

Summarizes some of the classic research on teacher education including some general aspects of program evaluation.

81. Lasley, Thomas J., ed. *Issues in Teacher Education*. Washington: American Association of Colleges for Teacher Education, 1986.

Presents eleven papers which address the historical and political perspectives of teacher education; the content and structure of teacher education programs; and mechanisms, including evaluation for creating quality teacher education programs.

82. Lasley, Thomas J., ed. *The Dynamics of Change in Teacher Education*. Washington: American Association of Colleges for Teacher Education, 1986.

Includes ten papers by outstanding educators and researchers addressing such topics as expectations and the school environment, the reform efforts, teacher induction, and the future of teacher education.

83. Lin, Bing. "An Anaylsis of the Selected Components of the Teacher Education Redesign Program at Kent State University." Ph.D. dissertation, Kent State University, 1982.

Analyzes selected components of the Teacher Education Redesign Program at Kent State University.

84. Madaus, George F., and others. *Evaluation Models: Viewpoints on Educational and Human Services*. Boston: Kluwer-Nijhoff Publishing Co., 1983.

Outlines a series of models for evaluating various aspects of teacher preparation programs.

85. McClain, Charles J. "Assessment Produces Degrees with Integrity." *Educational Record* 68 no. 1 (Winter 1987): 47-52.

    Describes a value-added assessment program at one institution that has been effective in aiding decision making and producing significant institutional change.

86. McEwing, Richard A. *Skills Related to Teaching: Perceived Importance and Mastery. 1980-81 Teacher Education Program Evaluation Study.* 1981. ERIC, ED 209 189.

    Describes the implementation of a model for the evaluation of teacher education programs at Idaho State University.

87. Medley, Donald M. *Teacher Competency and Teacher Effectiveness, A Review of Process-Product Research.* Washington, D. C.: American Association of Colleges for Teacher Education, 1977.

    Provides a review of the research on process-product research that is essential in designing an evaluation program for teacher education programs.

88. Minier, Judith Elaine. "An Evaluation of the Effectiveness of the Teacher Education Alternatives Model at St. Cloud State University." Ed.D. dissertation, The University of North Dakota, 1979.

    Describes an evaluation of the Teacher Education Alternatives Model Project used for training undergraduate elementary education students.

89. Moore, Kenneth D. "A Model for Teacher Preparation." *Contemporary Education* 59 no. 2 (Winter 1988): 104-109.

    Discusses the problems associated with the development and evaluation of teacher preparation programs.

90. Morris, Lynn Lyons, and Carol Taylor Fitz-Gibbon. *Evaluator's Handbook.* In *Program Evaluation Kit,* edited by Joan L. Herman. Beverly Hills, CA: Sage Publications, 1987.

Contains nine books designed to guide the planning and management of evaluations.

91. Nelli, Elizabeth, and Norma Nutter. *A Model for Evaluating Teacher Education Programs.* 1984. ERIC, ED 251 406.

Describes a comprehensive model for the evaluation of teacher education programs.

92. Nelson, David. *Assessment of Undergraduate Teacher Education at Saginaw Valley State University.* 1988. ERIC, ED 300 359.

Describes the implementation of an assessment model for undergraduate preservice teacher education programs at Saginaw Valley State University.

93. Novicki, Judith Rodriguez. "Description and Analysis of the Camp Lejune Teacher Education Consortium: A Modified Competency-Based Teacher Education Program." Ed.D. dissertation, The University of North Carolina at Greensboro, 1982.

Investigates whether a competency-based teacher education program could be modified through collaborative efforts involving several education agencies.

94. Oklahoma State Department of Education. *Accreditation Standards for Approved Teacher Education Programs.* 1984. ERIC, ED 251 421.

Reviews the revised standards for the state approval of teacher education programs in Oklahoma and more specifically the accreditation/evaluation process.

95. Oregon College of Education. *A Case Study: The Oregon College of Education, Teaching Research Division.* 1977. ERIC, ED 156 625.

Describes the evolution of the teacher education programs in the Oregon College of Education in Monmouth.

96. Pascarella, Frank John. "Graduate Education in Curriculum Planning: An Analysis." Ed.D. dissertation, State University of New York at Buffalo, 1980.

Discusses graduates' perceptions of their preparation for a Doctorate in Education in curriculum planning.

97. Patton, Michael Quinn. *Creative Evaluation.* Beverly Hills, CA: Sage Publications, 1987.

Outlines a variety of evaluation techniques that are applicable to teacher education programs.

98. Patton, Michael Quinn. *How to Use Qualitative Methods in Evaluation.* Newbury Park, CA: Sage Publications, 1987.

Outlines the use of qualitative methods in the evaluation of programs.

99. Perloff, Robert, and Evelyn Perloff, eds. *Values, Ethics, and Standards in Evaluation.* San Francisco: Jossey-Bass, 1980.

Consists of edited addresses, essays, and lectures dealing with evaluation research, social values, and program evaluation with application to teacher education programs.

100. Pfeiffer, William Wallace. "A Procedural Model for a Product Evaluation of the Teacher Education Program at the University of Idaho." Ph.D. dissertation, University of Idaho, 1980.

Describes a study to assess program objectives as measured by the National Teacher Examinations, the Minnesota Teacher Attitude Inventory, and the Teacher Appraisal Instrument.

101. Philosophy of Education Society. "Standards for Academic
     Professional Instruction in Philosophy of Education." *Educational
     Theory* 30 no. 4 (Fall 1980): 265-267.

     Describes guidelines for evaluating teacher education programs
     in terms of the : (1) qualifications of teachers of philosophy of
     education, (2) philosophical component of humanistic requirements
     for teacher certification, and (3) humanistic component of graduate
     programs.

102. Reed, Horace B. *The Accuracy-Meaning Tensions in Teacher
     Education Evaluation.* 1978. ERIC, ED 205 524.

     Examines the use of alternative approaches to the evaluation of
     teacher education programs.

103. Renney, James Edward. "A Formative Evaluation Study of the
     Professional Phase of the Pennsylvania State University's
     Secondary Education Program: Study 1.0." Ph.D. dissertation,
     The Pennsylvania State University, 1981.

     Summarizes evaluative data on the Pennsylvania State
     University's Undergraduate Secondary Education Program.

104. Rennie, Barbara Jean. "A College in Transition: New Approaches
     in Undergraduate Teacher Education." Ph.D. dissertation, Wayne
     State University, 1976.

     Analyzes the development, implementation, and evaluation of
     an undergraduate teacher education program at Wayne State
     University.

105. Richardson, Robert Lee Kenton. "Perceptions of Deans of
     Selected Colleges of Education Concerning The Improvement of
     Teacher Education Programs." Ph.D. dissertation, Southern
     Illinois University at Carbondale, 1985.

     Studies the effects of the national education report on teacher
     education reform and the recommendations of the deans concerning
     the quality of the preparation of preservice teachers.

106. Roth, Robert A. "Accreditation and Program Approval: Purposes and Varied Perspectives of Design." *Teacher Educator* 16 no. 3 (Winter 1980-81): 14-22.

     Discusses the issues related to program approval and accreditation at the state and national levels.

107. Sandefur, J. T. *An Illustrated Model for the Evaluation of Teacher Education Graduates.* 1970. ERIC, ED 080 485.

     Describes a follow-up model for the evaluation of teacher education programs.

108. Sanders, John Theodore. "The Winds of Change Influence NCATE: An Analysis of the NCATE Accreditation Process, 1979-1986." Ed.D. dissertation, The University of Nevada, Reno, 1987.

     Analyzes the NCATE accreditation decisions during 1979-1986 and the adoption and implementation of major changes in the standards.

109. Schumacher, Sally. *The Complexities of a Collaborative Teacher Education Program Evaluation.* 1985. ERIC, ED 261 985.

     Describes evaluation processes and procedures for a collaborative teacher education program are contrasted to those typically used in a cooperative teacher education program.

110. Sears, James T., and others. *Teacher Education Policies and Programs: Implementing Reform Proposals of the 1980's.* 1988. ERIC, ED 296 985.

     Examines the applications of educational reform proposals of the 1980's to teacher education programs and provides an extensive bibliography.

111. Sikula, John P., and Robert A. Roth. *Teacher Preparation and Certification: The Call for Reform.* Bloomington, IN: Phi Delta Kappa Foundation, 1984.

     Discusses changes in teacher education programs in four areas that need further evaluation: (1) national accreditation, (2) state program approval, (3) state certification, and (4) teacher preparation.

112. Simmons, Joanne Marie. "The Development of a Cost-Effectiveness Model For Evaluating Training Activities Within Teacher Education Programs." Ph.D. dissertation, Syracuse University, 1980.

　　　Discusses the development of a cost-effectiveness evaluation model and an analysis of how it can be best used by administrators and evaluators.

113. Smith, Nick L., ed. *New Techniques for Evaluation.* Beverly Hills: Sage Publications, 1981.

　　　Describes a variety of techniques and models useful in program evaluation including investigative journalism, art criticism, and cost analysis.

114. Smock, Richard, and Harold Hake. *A Systematic Approach to the Evaluation of Academic Departments.* 1977. ERIC, ED 146 180.

　　　Describes a system for the evaluation of each academic department at the University of Illinois at Urbana-Champaign.

115. South Carolina State Department of Education. *Policies, Procedures and Standards for the Approval of Teacher Education Programs in South Carolina.* 1986. ERIC, ED 278 666.

　　　Sets forth the specific policies and evaluation procedures that govern the approval of programs for the preparation of teachers in South Carolina.

116. Southern Regional Educational Board. *State-Level Evaluation of Teacher Education Programs in the SREB States.* Atlanta: Southern Regional Education Board, 1988.

　　　Outlines the state level processes for the approval of teacher education programs in states who are members of the Southern Regional Education Board.

117. Spillman, Russell J., and others. *A System for Assessing and Documenting the Experience of Pre/Inservice Teachers.* 1983. ERIC, ED 228 225.

     Looks at a continuing model for the evaluation of the teacher education programs at The Ohio State University.

118. Spradley, James P. *The Ethnographic Interview.* New York: Holt, Rinehart, and Winston, 1979.

     Outlines the use of ethnographic interview techniques that will have application in education evaluation.

119. Stedham, Donald J. *Improving Teacher Education: Academic Program Review.* 1980. ERIC, ED 205 467.

     Explores the quality of and ways to improve teacher education program evaluation.

120. Stufflebeam, Daniel L. *Conducting Educational Needs Assessments.* Boston: Kluwer-Nijhoff Publishing, 1984.

     Outlines procedures for conducting an educational needs assessment; includes practical examples, instruments, procedures and analysis, and schemes for reporting the results of the work.

121. Tamblyn, Carolyn Knight. "A Study of the Development of Standards For Teacher Preparation and Certification in Alabama." Ed.D. dissertation, Auburn University, 1983.

     Examines the origin and development of standards for teacher education and certification in Alabama.

122. Wagner, Irma Guzman. "State Mandated Educational Evaluations: Toward an Evaluation Delivery Model." Ph.D. dissertation, Claremont Graduate School, 1976.

     Analyzes the state mandated evaluations of teacher education programs in California and makes suggestions for an evaluation delivery model.

123. Wang, Margaret C., and Herbert J. Walbert. "Evaluating
     Educational Programs: An Integrative, Causal-modeling
     Approach." *Educational Evaluation and Policy Analysis* 5 no. 3
     (Fall 1983): 347-366.

   Presents a case for the use of causal models derived from a
   substantive knowledge base of theory and research in the evaluation
   of educational programs.

124. Warmbrod, Catharine P. and Jon J. Persavich. *Postsecondary*
     Program Evaluation. 1981. ERIC, ED 227 362.

   Outlines a comprehensive model for postsecondary program
   evaluation that includes evaluation materials, utilization,
   instrumentation and interviewing, consultative team evaluations,
   advisory committee perceptions, administrative and supervisory
   personnel perceptions, instructor perceptions, current student
   perceptions, follow-up with former students and employers, cost
   analysis evaluation, and preparing and reporting results.

125. Webster, David S. *How to Assess Quality in Master's Degree*
     Programs--A New and Better Way. 1979. ERIC, ED 185 916.

   Examines a system for the evaluation of programs for the
   preparation of teachers at the master's degree level.

126. Wilkerson, Judy Rothgeeser. "SIDPASS, An Accreditation Self-
     Study Model With An Initial Application To The National Council
     for Accreditation of Teacher Education." Ph.D. dissertation,
     University of South Florida, 1987.

   Describes a model process for conducting the accreditation self-
   study for the National Council for Accreditation of Teacher
   Education.

127. Wittrock, Merlin C. ed. *Handbook of Research on Teaching.*
     New York: Macmillan Publishing Co., 1986.

   Includes a collection of 35 papers with extensive bibliographies
   on the status of research on teaching.

128. Worthen, Blaine R., and James R. Sanders. *Educational Evaluation: Alternative Approaches and Practical Guidelines*. New York: Longman, 1987.

Provides an overview of educational evaluation and outlines various approaches for conducting process and product evaluations of educational programs.

129. Worthen, Blaine R., and Karl R. White. *Evaluating Educational and Social Programs: Guidelines for Proposal Review, Onsite Evaluation, Evaluation Contracts, and Technical Assistance*. Boston: Kluwer-Nijhoff Publishing, 1987.

Outlines practical approaches to the evaluation of educational and social programs including such areas as review of proposals, evaluation models, statistical analysis, and providing technical assistance.

130. Yang, Zhi-Ling. "An Analysis of the Goals and Intents of the Teacher Education Redesign Program at Kent State University." Ph.D. dissertation, Kent State University, 1982.

Explores the goals of the Teacher Education Redesign Program at Kent State University.

131. Yeany, Russell H. "Redefining Process and Product in Teacher Training: Alternative Modes for Evaluating Teacher Training Programs." *Journal of Research in Science Teaching* 17 no. 5 (September 1980): 383-386.

Examines alternative evaluation models to expand the concept of process-product research in teaching preparation programs.

132. Zimpher, Nancy L., and William E. Loadman. *A Documentation and Assessment System for Student Program Evaluation*. 1986. ERIC, ED 264 192.

Describes a comprehensive system for evaluation of teacher education programs used at The Ohio State University.

II. KNOWLEDGE BASE AND QUALITY CONTROLS

133. Adams, Ronald D. *A Survey of AACTE Member Institutions Regarding Change in Teacher Education Practice to Improve the Quality of Graduates*. 1983. ERIC, ED 237 494.

   Reports the results of a survey of practices to improve the quality of teacher education programs.

134. American Association of Colleges for Teacher Education. *Educating a Profession: Extended Programs for Teacher Education*. 1983. ERIC, ED 236 139.

   Considers the need for extended teacher education programs and the associated knowledge base.

135. Antonelli, George A. *The Educational Warranty: Redesigning the Profession*. 1986. ERIC, ED 267 043.

   Provides a description of a program which guarantees the quality of a teacher education program through evaluation.

136. Arnold, D. S., and others. *Quality Control in Teacher Education: Some Policy Issues*. Washington, D. C.: American Association of Colleges for Teacher Education, 1977.

   Investigates some of the issues in providing quality controls in teacher education programs.

137. Bedics, Richard A. *Program Mapping: Quality Control for Academic Programs*. 1984. ERIC, ED 257 524.

   Presents mapping as a means of providing quality controls in teacher education programs.

138. Behling, Herman E. *Quality Control of Teacher Preparation Programs Through the Program Approval Process.* 1984. ERIC, ED 250 300.

Provides an analysis of reports from evaluation teams that have reviewed teacher education programs.

139. Birch, Derek W., and Craig F. Johnson. *Quality Control/Assurance in Post Secondary Education: An Outcomes Approach.* 1988. ERIC, ED 298 859.

Summarizes the quality control and quality assurance practices in six teacher preparation programs.

140. Clemens, Thomas D. *The Dissemination and Utilization of Research and Development in Education--Two Strategies.* 1976. ERIC, ED 117 859.

Describes systems for maintaining and improving the knowledge base of teacher education and for disseminating information.

141. Daiber, Robert A. "Technology Education and Its Contribution to General Education." *Journal of Epsilon Pi Tau* 5 no. 2 (Fall 1979): 40-43.

Explores the need for a common knowledge base about technology education.

142. Defino, Maria E., and Heather Carter, eds. *Changing Teacher Practices.* 1982. ERIC, ED 223 582.

Discusses changing practices in teacher education and the need for the development and evaluation of an adequate knowledge base.

143. Ditosto, Evelyn, and Eugene Huddle, eds. *Alternative Programs in Teacher Education.* 1977. ERIC, ED 163 006.

Explores practices and patterns in evaluation and the knowledge base of teacher education.

144. Dottin, Erskine S., and others. *The Conceptual Framework for the Teacher Education Program at the University of West Florida.* 1987. ERIC, ED 283 783.

Describes the knowledge base upon which the teacher education program at the University of West Florida was developed.

145. Doyle, Walter. "Effective Teaching and the Concept of Master Teacher." *Elementary School Journal* 86 no. 1 (September 1985): 27-34.

Focuses on issues related to using recent information from research and evaluation as a knowledge base for making decisions about teacher mastery.

146. Flippo, Rona F. *Teacher Certification Testing Across the United States and a Consideration of Some of the Issues.* 1985. ERIC, ED 260 115.

Presents issues in assuring quality controls in teacher education programs.

147. Georgia Professional Standards Commission. *Status of Teacher Education as It Relates to Critical Issues in Georgia.* 1983. ERIC, ED 237 487.

Describes teacher education program evaluation in Georgia and the determination of the needed knowledge base.

148. Gibbs, Forbes, and Blaise Cronin. "Prototype Identification Using a Knowledge-Base Management System." *Education for Information* 3 no. 4 (December 1985): 307-312.

Describes Expert 4, a knowledge-base management system which develops student performance predictors based on routinely collected data.

149. Gideonse, Hendrik D. "Blackwell's Commentaries, Engineering's Handbooks, and Merck's Manuals: What Would a Teacher's Equivalent Be?" *Educational Evaluation and Policy Analysis* 8 no. 3 (Fall 1986): 316-323.

Indicates that knowledge bases for teaching ought to be reflected not only in teacher education but also be readily available in resources such as a "teacher's handbook."

150. Gideonse, Hendrick D. *Relating Knowledge to Teacher Education: Responding to NCATE's Knowledge Base and Related Standards.* Washington: American Association of Colleges for Teacher Education, 1989.

Explains the rationale for knowledge based curricula in teacher education programs, describes necessary kinds of knowledge, clarifies the NCATE standards, and describes compliance strategies relative to the accreditation standards.

151. Glazer, Judith S. *The Master's Degree. Tradition, Diversity, Innovation.* 1986. ERIC, ED 279 260.

Summarizes research on the master's degree and discusses the issues related to quality control.

152. Hatfield, Robert C., and Sherry Ralston. *Professional Assessment and Development.* 1978. ERIC, ED 186 368.

Proposes a paradigm for conceptualizing and studying professional development that could lead teachers and researchers to greater effectiveness in facilitating teacher improvement.

153. Johnston, John M. *The Knowledge Base for Teacher Induction.* 1988. ERIC, ED 291 722.

Cites articles and reports of studies on the subject of beginning teacher induction.

154. Johnston, John M., and Kevin Ryan. *Research on the Beginning Teacher: Implications for Teacher Education.* 1980. ERIC, ED 209 188.

Explores the knowledge base about the induction of beginning teachers and suggests evaluation techniques that can be used.

155. Jones, Donald W. "Assessing the Knowledge Base in Teacher Education: A Fundamental and Necessary Task." *Teacher Education Quarterly* 15 no. 2 (Spring 1988): 20-31.

Examines the need for adequate methods for assessing the knowledge base in teacher education.

156. Martorella, Peter H. *Standards for Secondary Social Studies Teacher Education Programs.* 1977. ERIC, ED 146 109.

Describes the development of quality controls in programs for the preparation of social studies teachers.

157. Medley, Donald M. "Research in Teacher Effectiveness--Where It Is and How It Got Here." *Journal of Classroom Interaction* 13 no. 2 (1978): 16-21.

Discusses the construction of and evaluation of a knowledge base for teacher education programs.

158. Reynolds, Maynard C., ed. *Knowledge Base for the Beginning Teacher* New York: Pergamon Press, 1989.

Discusses the state-of-the-art of the knowledge base for beginning teachers.

159. Sears, James T. "A Critical Ethnography of Teacher Education Programs at Indiana University: An Inquiry into the Perceptions of Students and Faculty Regarding Quality and Effectiveness." Ph.D. dissertation, Indiana University, 1984.

Describes a two year study which investigates the frames of reference held by students and faculty toward the undergraduate teacher training curriculum at Indiana University-Bloomington.

160. Seeley, John A. "Program Review and Evaluation." *New Directions for Institutional Research* 31 (September 1981): 45-60.

Describes ways that evaluation of teacher education programs can affect the knowledge base.

161. Short, Edmund C. "Curriculum Decision Making in Teacher Education: Policies, Program Development, and Design." *Journal of Teacher Education* 38 no. 4 (July/August 1987): 2-12.

Outlines processes of curriculum development, policy making, and program development in teacher education that have significant relationship to the concept of a knowledge base.

162. Shulman, Lee S. "Knowledge and Teaching: Foundations of the New Reform." *Harvard Educational Review* 57 no. 1 (1987): 1-22.

Examines some of the major issues related to the development and evaluation of a knowledge base for teacher education programs.

163. Smith, David C. *Developing Operation PROTEACH.* 1980. ERIC, ED 213 681.

Describes operation PROTEACH, a teacher preparation program at the University of Florida.

164. Troutt, William Earl. "The Quality Assurance Function of Regional Accreditation." Ph.D. dissertation, George Peabody College for Teachers, 1978.

Studies the literature on college impact to identify institutional characteristics associated with educational quality and accreditation standards.

165. Valli, L., and Alan R. Tom. "How Adequate are the Knowledge Base Frameworks in Teacher Education?" *Journal of Teacher Education* 39 no. 5 (September/October): 5-12.

Suggests criteria for use in assessing knowledge base frameworks including scholarly papers, professional association guidelines and documents, and teacher education programs.

166. Webb, L. Dean. *Teacher Evaluation.* 1983. ERIC, ED 240 661.

Discusses legal standards relative to the evaluation of the knowledge base of teacher education programs.

167. Wisniewski, Richard. "Illinois Smith and the Secret of the Knowledge Base." *Journal of Teacher Education* 39 no. 5 (September/October 1988): 2-4.

Presents an allegorical view of the knowledge base for teacher education in its broadest perspective.

III. STUDENTS

Admissions

168. Aksamit, Donna, and others. "Relationships Between PPST and
ACT Scores and Their Implications for the Basic Skills Testing of
Prospective Teachers." *Journal of Teacher Education* 38 no. 6
(November/December 1987): 48-52.

Uses a canonical correlation analysis and application of double-
cross validation procedures to provide evidence of significant shared
variance between the Pre-Professional Skills Test and the American
College Test scores of 537 education majors questioning the need
for students to take both tests.

169. American Association of Colleges for Teacher Education. *Teacher
Education Policy in the States: 50-State Survey of Legislative and
Administrative Actions.* 1985. ERIC, ED 257 833.

Reviews the nine areas of a State Issues Clearinghouse
established by the American Association of Colleges for Teacher
Education and includes standards for admission to teacher education
programs, incentives for students to enter teaching, alternative
certification models, program curricula, program capacity, program
resources, faculty, inservice opportunities, and evidence of equity.

170. Amodeo, Luiza B., and Jeanette Martin. *Search for Quality: The
Sophomore Diagnostic Screening Process in the Teacher
Preparation Program at New Mexico State University.* 1982.
ERIC, ED 217 045.

Describes the New Mexico State University's College of
Education's admission screening process which consists of three
parts, including successful completion of prescribed courses,

achieving satisfactory scores on a series of diagnostic tests, and
assessment of teaching potential.

171. Anderson, Betty, and others. *The Impact of State Mandated
     Testing on Teacher Education in Florida.* 1986. ERIC, ED 270
     418.

     Discusses state mandated testing in Florida and its impact on
     admission to teacher education programs, accreditation of programs,
     state approval of programs, and the impact on teacher education in
     general.

172. Antes, Richard L. *Teacher Education Admission Testing:
     Development and Implementation.* 1985. ERIC, ED 272 498.

     Consists of a monograph on competency assessment,
     competency test development, competency testing for admission
     into teacher education programs, costs of basic skills testing, and
     evaluating standardized tests.

173. Applegate, Jane H. "Teacher Candidate Selection: An Overview."
     Journal of Teacher Education 38 no. 2 (March/April 1987): 2-6.

     Reviews four basic issues related to candidate selection, purpose
     of the selection, standards and criteria for selection, professional
     judgment of teacher candidates, and legal and ethical considerations
     of the selection process.

174. Ashburn, Elizabeth A., and Robert L. Fisher. *Methods of
     Assessing Teacher Education Students.* 1984. ERIC, ED 255
     493.

     Summarizes the results of a conference of educators convened to
     consider methods of evaluating teacher education students which
     focused on the relationships between candidate quality and teacher
     effectiveness.

175. Astin, Alexander W., and others. *The American Freshman: Twenty Year Trends, 1966-1985.* 1987. ERIC, ED 279 279.

   Presents results of the Cooperative Institutional Research Programs' annual surveys of college freshmen since 1966 which provide useful information relative to the potential supply of students who may desire to enter a teacher preparation program.

176. Barak, Amiah. "Characteristics of Teacher Education Students." Ph.D. dissertation, The Ohio State University, 1979.

   Lists the characteristics of students who intend to major in teacher education and summarizes the qualification of those who successfully complete programs of study.

177. Barbe, Richard, and others. *A Statewide Teacher Education Needs Assessment.* 1984. ERIC, ED 246 042.

   Presents a needs assessment model developed in Georgia.

178. Barnes, Carol P., and Dennis B. Tierney. *California's Problems in Operationalizing the Quest for Quality in Teacher Education.* 1983. ERIC, ED 235 172.

   Outlines the admission processes for teacher preparation programs in California's colleges and universities.

179. Benner, Susan, and others. "Admission Boards: The Contribution of Professional Judgment to the Admission Process." *Journal of Teacher Education* 38 no. 2 (March/April 1987): 7-11.

   Describes the use of admissions procedures in the teacher education program at the University of Tennessee that entail higher quantitative and additional qualitative standards, including the use of admission boards which make final admission decisions.

180. Berkshire, Jacqueline, and Douglas Yarbrough. "An Examination of PPST Performance of Transfer and Nontransfer Students." *Teacher Education and Practice* 4 no. 1 (Spring/Summer 1987): 51-54.

   Compares the performance on the Pre-Professional Skills Test of transfer students with nontransfer students and the performance of transfer students from two-year institutions with those from four-year institutions.

181. Brady-Ciampa, Bartholomew. *Academic Performance and Underlying Personality Predispositions of Provincial vs. Regional Graduate Students.* 1981. ERIC, ED 212 576.

Compares academic and attitudinal differences between students working toward the master's degree in teacher education who had obtained their undergraduate degrees at other institutions with a group who had obtained their degrees at the same institution where they were working on their advanced degrees.

182. Brinkley, W. L., Jr. "The True Role of Tests in Admissions Decisions." *NASSP Bulletin* 67 no. 460 (February 1983): 60-64.

Discusses the actual uses to which achievement test scores are put in the college admissions process and factors that should be considered when treating test scores as admissions criteria.

183. Brubaker, Harold A. "Selection and Retention in Teacher Education: A Model." *Teacher Educator* 12 no. 1 (1976): 17-25.

Describes the development of a model for improving selection-retention procedures in teacher education, criteria for admission to the profession, role of student personnel services, and provisions for probationary status, performance components, and feedback.

184. Burrows, Charles Milburn. "A Study of Admissions and Retention Criteria in Teacher Education Programs." Ph.D. dissertation, The University of Oklahoma, 1976.

Investigates the differences in criteria used in admission and retention of students in teacher education programs at various types of institutions.

185. California Commission of Teacher Credentialing. *CBEST Performance in Relation to Personal Background Factors.* 1984. ERIC, ED 242 666.

Reports the development of the California Basic Educational Skills Test and its use as a screening device for admission to teacher education programs.

186. Carlson, Robert E. *The Impact on Preparation Institutions of Competency Tests for Educators.* 1985. ERIC, ED 258 968.

    Explores the changes that have been made in teacher preparation programs as a result of the increased emphasis on competency testing by the states.

187. Cobb, Donald K., and others. *Selecting Teachers: An Effective Model.* 1984. ERIC, ED 241 464.

    Reviews the Kentucky plan for the admission of candidates to teacher education programs based on a multifaceted selection/retention process.

188. Collins, Mary Lynn, and others. *Teacher Candidate Selection and Evaluation.* ERIC, ED 219 379.

    Focuses on entry level criteria for acceptance into a teacher education program, levels of competence a candidate should demonstrate, legal implications of screening, criteria for denial of admission to teacher education and comparison of grades in teacher education programs with those in other areas.

189. Daly, Richard F. *A Comparative Study of the Pre-Professional Skills Test (PPST) Test Scores of Pre-Service Teachers at Mankato State University.* 1987. ERIC, ED 291 630.

    Discusses the results of a comparison of male and female teacher education candidates' scores on the Pre-Professional Skills Test.

190. deFelix, Judith Walker, and Robert W. Houston. *Implications of Entrance Requirements for Success in Graduate Teacher Education Programs.* 1986. ERIC, ED 293 848.

    Examines the admission requirements for entry into a master's degree program in education and makes comparisons between two different groups of students.

191. Duke, Charles R. "Developing a Writing Assessment of
     Candidates for Admission to Teacher Education." *Journal of
     Teacher Education* 36 no. 2 (March/April 1985): 7-11.

        Indicates that many students entering teacher education
     programs are deficient in writing skills and explores ways to
     overcome the problem.

192. Dupuis, Mary M., and Edward R. Fagan. *The Basic Skills of
     Prospective Teachers: How Well Do They Read/Write/Speak?*
     1983. ERIC, ED 247 226.

        Describes the basic assessment system for admission to teacher
     education programs at the Pennsylvania State University.

193. Eckart, Joyce A. *Does the Use of Quantitative Criteria for
     Restricted Admissions Imply No Subjective Judgement?* 1988.
     ERIC, ED 299 225.

        Describes the efforts undertaken by the elementary education
     department at the medium sized mid-western state university to
     create and implement a restrictive admissions process that includes
     the establishment of minimum cut scores on standardized tests.

194. Etheridge, Carol P. *Student Perspective of the Lyndhurst
     Program: Cycle I.* 1986. ERIC, ED 280 839.

        Reports the admission steps used in the Lyndhurst Program
     (fifth year program) at Memphis State University.

195. Etheridge, Carol P. *The Students' Perspective: MAT Program
     Cycle I.* 1986. ERIC, ED 280 838.

        Outlines the admission steps used in the master's program in
     teacher education at Memphis State University and describes the
     characteristics of the individuals initially admitted to the program.

196. Fisher, Robert L., and Marilyn E. Feldman. "Trends in Standards for Admission to Teacher Education." *Action in Teacher Education* 6 no. 4 (Winter 1984/85): 59-63.

Reports the results of a survey of 530 institutions to determine the requirements being used for admission to teacher education programs.

197. Gallegos, Arnold M., and Harry Gibson. "Are We Sure the Quality of Teacher Candidates is Declining?" *Phi Delta Kappan* 64 no. 1 (September 1982): 33.

Reports that self-selection is weeding out the poorer students in the teacher education programs at Western Washington University and that although the grade point average of freshman is declining for the university, it is rising in teacher education.

198. Gans, Thomas G. *Students' Performance in M. Ed. Programs at the Cleveland State University, 1968-1975.* 1976. ERIC, ED 131 053.

Looks at the performance of students in the M.Ed. programs at Cleveland State University based on patterns of admission and student characteristics.

199. Garcia, Peter A. *A Study of Teacher Competency Testing and Test Validity with Implications for Minorities and the Results and Implications of the Use of the Pre-Professional Skills Test (PPST) as a Screening Device for Entrance into Teacher Education Programs in Texas.* 1985. ERIC, ED 270 389.

Discusses the failure of minority groups to achieve admission to teacher education programs and reports the results of a study of the use of the Pre-Professional Skills Test in Texas.

200. Goertz, Margaret, and others. *The Impact of State Policy on Entrance into the Teaching Profession.* 1984. ERIC, ED 255 515.

Reports a study of the 50 states regarding policies of admission of individuals into teacher education programs and the teaching profession.

201. Griffin, Annette Teer. "The Relationships Between College
      Aptitude, Race, College Hours Completed, and P-PST Scores For
      Education Students in Texas Public Colleges and Universities."
      Ed.D. dissertation, North Texas State University, 1985.

      Reports the relationships between scores on the P-PST and
      college aptitude tests with the race of the student and the number of
      college hours earned at the time of testing.

202. Guyton, Edith, and Elizabeth Farokhi. "Relationships Among
      Academic Performance, Basic Skills, Subject Matter Knowledge,
      and Teaching Skills of Teacher Education Graduates." *Journal of
      Teacher Education* 38 no. 5 (September/October 1987): 37-42.

      Discusses the relationship among academic performance, basic
      skills testing, subject matter knowledge, and teaching skills of
      graduates and concludes that many trends in current educational
      practice are not based on sound research.

203. Halpin, Glennelle, and Gerald Halpin. "Setting Performance
      Standards: A Documentation and Discussion." *Education* 103 no.
      2 (Winter 1982): 118-128.

      Presents step-by-step procedures used to set minimum
      competency standards in English for admission to teacher education
      at a large university.

204. Heard, Sharon A., and Jerry B. Ayers. "Validity of the American
      College Test in Predicting Success on the Pre-Professional Skills
      Test." *Educational and Psychological Measurement* 48 no. 2
      (Spring 1988): 197-200.

      Examines the use of the American College Test as a predictor
      of scores on the Pre-Professional Skills Test for students for
      admission to a teacher education program.

205. Hoffman, Hubert A., and others. "Selective Admissions: A First
      Step in Professional Preparation." *Journal of Physical Education
      and Recreation* 46 no. 8 (1975): 29-30.

      Discusses the use of selective admissions for a professional
      physical education program.

206. Hopkins, Scott. *Basic Skills Tests in Teacher Education: A Shift from the Three R's to the Two C's.* 1986. ERIC, ED 267 061.

   Addresses responsibility for developing and using admissions tests, cost of tests, legal and/or moral responsibilities to the profession, societal implications of admission testing, and types of tests (basic skills, norm referenced, and criterion referenced).

207. Hypes, Margaret Ann. "Admission, Retention, and Exit Criteria for Students in Teacher Education Programs in Tennessee." Ed.D. dissertation, The University of Tennessee, 1988.

   Discusses the admission, retention and exit criteria for teacher education students in the State of Tennessee.

208. Illinois State Board of Education. *Institutional Assessment of Prospective Educational Personnel in Undergraduate Programs. A Study to Assess the Quality of the Preparation and Performance of Educational Personnel.* 1982. ERIC, ED 262 486.

   Reports the results of a five part survey of institutions of higher education relative to admission to teacher education programs in five areas, including admission to the institution, admission to education programs, admission to student teaching, graduation and recommendation for licensure, and general perspective of the program.

209. Ishler, Richard E. "Research Brief--Teacher Effectiveness and Grade Point Averages: A Profile of Master Teachers." *Texas Tech Journal of Education* 9 no. 3 (Fall 1982): 215-217.

   Questions whether the requirement of a 2.5 grade point average for admission to teacher education programs or for certification will improve teaching.

210. Johnson, James Thomas. "A Canonical Correlational Analysis of the College Outcome Measures Program and Other Variables Used For Admission and Certification in Teacher Education Programs in Mississippi." Ph.D. dissertation, University of Southern Mississippi, 1986.

      Assesses the efficacy of the College Outcome Measures Program as a pre-admission screening device for education majors in the state of Mississippi.

211. Johnson, Joyce Williams. "A Survey of Admission Standards for Elementary Teacher Education Programs in the Southeastern Land-Grant and State Institutions." Ph.D. dissertation, University of Pittsburgh, 1986.

      Investigates the requirements used for admission to elementary teacher education programs of southeastern land-grant and state institutions.

212. Kamaka, Elissa. "Model-Netics: Implications for and Approaches to the Selection of Candidates in a Teacher Education Program at a Small Private Liberal Arts College." Ph.D. dissertation, Saint Louis University, 1981.

      Reports the use of the Model-Netics Program of Main Event Management Corporation for the selection process of candidates in the teacher education program of a small private liberal arts college.

213. Kapel, David E., and others. *Psychological and Social/Emotional Fitness for Teacher Education Students: A National Survey of Current Practices.* 1988. ERIC, ED 293 850.

      Examines the issue of practice standards relative to establishing psychological and social/emotional fitness of candidates for admission to teacher education programs.

214. King, Ruth, and Marlene Bireley. *Undergraduate Selection/Retention in Wright State University's College of Education and Human Services.* 1982. ERIC, ED 220 458.

      Examines the use of a mentor system in the selection/retention process at a state university and describes the success and limitations of the program.

215. Kline, Kathleen Ann Klus. "Relationship Between Scores on the American College Test (ACT) and Grade Point Averages in Selected Groups of Prospective Teachers and Business Majors." Ed.D. dissertation, East Texas State University, 1984.

Compares the relationship between ACT composite scores and grade point averages in a select group of prospective teachers and business majors.

216. Knight, J. Pat. *Who Shall Control Entry to Teacher Education? North Carolina Quality Assurance Program.* 1981. ERIC, ED 209 225.

Describes the two major premises of the North Carolina Quality Assurance Program: crucial competencies for teacher effectiveness can be identified, verified, and validated; and teacher education begins at entry and progresses in an orderly and sequential manner to graduation.

217. Laman, Archie E., and Dorothy E. Reeves. *A Survey of Criteria for Admitting Students to Teacher Education Programs.* 1982. ERIC, ED 220 433.

Describes a survey of member institutions of the American Association of Colleges for Teacher Education to ascertain the criteria for admitting students to teacher education programs.

218. Mallery, Anne L., and others. *Assessment of Preservice Teachers in Six Pennsylvania Colleges and Universities.* 1983. ERIC, ED 240 115.

Describes a study identifying reading competency standards for students seeking admission to Pennsylvania teacher education programs.

219. Marshall, J. Dan, and others. *The Recruitment and Induction of "Quality" Students Into Teacher Education: A Case Study.* 1988. ERIC, ED 294 843.

    Discusses findings from the first two years of a six-year longitudinal study related to the recruitment, training, and retention of quality students into teaching and indicates that sustained or extended recruitment is a way to develop and monitor students' introduction to the teaching profession.

220. Marshall, John D., and others., *The Brackenridge Internship in Teaching Program: Acknowledging Research as a Component of Teacher Education Reform.* 1987. ERIC, ED 277 679.

    Reports results of the Brackenridge Internship in Teaching Program's three overlapping stages: acclimation—recognition of the scholars as a group from which much is expected and providing leadership for them; early specialization and introduction into teaching; and development of a sense of professionalism.

221. Marshman, Larry R. *Teacher Education Program Admission--A Case Analysis.* 1981. ERIC, ED 210 249.

    Analyzes the admission requirements for teacher education programs in the State of Louisiana.

222. McCurdy, Katheleen Brassey. "Concerns Regarding Teaching Among Students Entering and Exiting a Teacher Education Program." Ph.D. dissertation, University of Idaho, 1982.

    Investigates the concerns of education students and determines whether differences in student's majors and levels of preparedness influence outcome variables.

223. Mercer, Walter A. "Teacher Education Admission Requirements: Alternatives for Black Prospective Teachers and Other Minorities." *Journal of Teacher Education* 35 no. 1 (January/February 1984): 26-29.

    Outlines reasons for providing alternative standards for admission into teacher education programs for Blacks and other minorities who do not attain satisfactory scores on entrance examinations.

224. Neuweiler, Hilary B. *Teacher Education Policy in the States: A 50-State Survey of Legislative and Administrative Actions.* 1988. ERIC, ED 296 997.

    Summarizes and updates previous studies of the state policies relative to admission to teacher education programs and for entry into the teaching profession.

225. Pugach, Marleen C., and James D. Raths. "Testing Teachers: Analysis and Recommendations." *Journal of Teacher Education* 34 no. 1 (January/February 1983): 37-43.

    Addresses two central aspects of the teacher-testing movement, the assumptions that form the basis for the prescription that teachers should be tested, and the various domains in which testing might take place; recommendations are made for the use of competency tests.

226. Reuter, Steven, F., and Rene D. Hersrud. *University of Minnesota Postbaccalureate Teacher Candidate Selection: An Admissions Perspective.* 1988. ERIC, ED 290 753.

    Describes in detail the selection process and admission procedures for students who enter a postbaccalaureate teacher preparation program at the University of Minnesota.

227. Robbins, Jerry H. *Comments on Grade Point Average for Admission to Teacher and Administrator Preparation Programs.* 1985. ERIC, ED 256 720.

    Discusses the pros and cons of raising grade point average admission requirements for undergraduate and graduate teacher education programs for individuals preparing for administrative positions (i.e., principals, supervisors, and superintendents).

228. Rudner, Lawrence M. "Teacher Testing-An Update." *Educational Measurement* 7 no. 1 (Spring 1988): 16-19.

    Discusses the issues related to screening unqualified individuals from entering preparation programs and teaching, strengthening the profession, attracting better qualified candidates, and restoring public confidence; also outlines the testing programs in effect in each of the states.

229. Sandefur, J. T. *Competency Assessment of Teachers: The 1984 Report.* 1984. ERIC, ED 256 716.

   Describes the competency assessment of teachers and teacher candidates and provides a summary of the types of tests being used.

230. Sandefur, J. T. *Standards for Admission to Teacher Education Programs.* 1984. ERIC, ED 251 417.

   Provides an analysis of the increasingly stringent admissions criteria on students seeking to enter teacher preparation programs, analyzes the impact of new requirements, and discusses the advantages and disadvantages of the policies.

231. Sandefur, J. T. "Standards for Admission to Teacher Education Programs." *Journal of Human Behavior and Learning* 3 no. 1 (Spring 1986): 3-19.

   Examines standards for admission to teacher education programs as mandated by individual states and what the effects have been on programs, faculty, students, and the public.

232. Schlecty, Phillip C., and Victor S. Vance. "Recruitment, Selection, and Retention: The Shape of the Teaching Force." *Elementary School Journal* 83 no. 4 (March 1983): 469-487.

   Reviews patterns of teacher recruitment, selection, and retention from 1950-70 that are essential to understanding the shape of the present teaching corps and its future characteristics over the next decade.

233. Schlechty, Phillip C., and Victor S. Vance. *Recruitment, Selection and Retention: The Shape of the Teaching Force.* 1982. ERIC, ED 221 541.

   Outlines some issues relative to the recruitment, selection, and retention of teachers in teacher education programs.

234. Scott, Jean A. "How the College Admissions Process Really Works." *NASSP Bulletin* 67 no. 460 (February 1983): 47-59.

   Describes the range of policies, criteria, and weightings used in the process of selecting among candidates for admission in 19 public and private colleges and universities and notes the need for adequate communications between colleges and the schools previously attended.

235. Smith, Eugene. *Who Shall Teach English?* 1984. ERIC, ED 249 498.

Examines a unique screening procedure that potential secondary English candidates undergo prior to admission to a teacher education program.

236. Stark, James G. "A Study of the Correlation Between Certain Entry Level Characteristics of Teacher Candidates and Their Performance Rating For Student Teaching." Ed.D. dissertation, United States International University, 1983.

Investigates whether a relationship existed between the performance scores of 60 student teachers and their scores on twelve independent variables. Students attended Christian Heritage College in El Cajon, CA.

237. Stevens, Dorothy Jo. "A Study of Relationships Between Prospective Teacher Selection and Student Teacher Performance." Ph.D. dissertation, The University of Nebraska-Lincoln, 1978.

Summarizes a study conducted to determine if two selected instruments and the grade point average used in teacher candidate selection were significantly related to three selected criterion employed in ascertaining student teacher performance.

238. Stoker, W. M., and Miguel Tarrab. *A Study of the Relationship of Pre-Professional Skills Tests and American College Tests.* 1984. ERIC, ED 252 496.

Examines the use of the Pre-Professional Skills Test as an admission screening device for teacher education programs and concludes that scores from the test are correlated with scores from the American College Tests.

239. Sykes, Gary. "Teacher Preparation and the Teacher Workforce: Problems and Prospects for the 80s." *American Education* 19 no. 2 (March 1983): 23-29.

Highlights evidence concerning teacher preparation and recruitment, including academic ability, entry and retention in teaching, mismatched supply and demand, inadequate rewards, quality, and controversy in the teacher education programs, and approaches to reform.

240. Teshome, Almaz. "The Relationships of Test of Basic Skills To Characteristics of Teacher Education Candidates." Ed.D. dissertation, Northern Illinois University, 1985.

Studies the relationship between the Tests of Basic Skills and the variables of race, gender, major, transfer versus native student, GPA, and ACT composite scores of students admitted to teacher education programs.

241. Thayer, Louis. "Toward a More Person-Centered Approach in Teacher Education." *Education* 101 no. 4 (Summer 1981): 322-329.

Explains a process model which is based on trainee input and is especially designed to help trainees learn basic interpersonal relationship skills, review program and professional expectations and opportunities, assess their potential and motivation for different careers in teaching and related professions, and examine their career objectives.

242. Theodossin, Ernest. *Selection Through Interviewing: Entrance Procedures in Teacher Recruitment.* 1983. ERIC, ED 267 036.

Looks at the process and procedures of interviewing to select individuals to enter teacher preparation programs and presents interviewing forms and references.

243. Uno, T., and others. "Admission Criteria of Undergraduate Teacher Preparation." *Education* 101 no. 4 (Summer 1981): 315-321.

   Analyzes multiple selection criteria for teacher preparation programs in several states and relates them to institutional factors such as student enrollment and funding sources.

244. Van Devender, Evelyn McDonald. "Standards For Entering Teacher Education Programs: A Comparative Analysis of Selected Educators' Opinions." Ph.D. dissertation, University of Southern Mississippi, 1982.

   Surveys the opinions of university faculty and elementary and secondary teachers on the requirements for admission into teacher education programs.

245. Vargas, Quintin, III. *Policy Recommendations for Teacher Education in Texas.* 1983. ERIC, ED 238 864.

   Presents observations relative to the Texas legislation requiring the passing of an admission test before entering a teacher preparation program and additional testing prior to receiving a license to teach.

246. Vasek, Richard J., and Arnold J. Moore. *Managing Students' Progress through Teacher Education Program.* 1985. ERIC, ED 266 092.

   Presents an outline of streamlined student record-keeping, admission procedures, and advisement processes for those admitted to teacher education programs.

247. Wakeford, Mary E. *The Incremental Predictive Validity of NTE Communication Skills and General Knowledge Tests Used for Admission to Teacher Education and Implications for Policy.* 1988. ERIC, ED 293 874.

   Discusses the validity of the National Teacher Examinations Communication Skills and General Knowledge tests as admissions criteria for teacher education programs.

248. Watkins, J. Foster, and Ronnie L. Standford. *ACT Scores and Selective Admissions: An Exploratory Look at Some One-Time Data.* 1983. ERIC, ED 230 520.

    Examines the impact of state mandated admission criteria to teacher education programs in Alabama and the impact of exit examinations required for initial licensure.

249. Watts, Doyle. "Admissions Standards for Teacher Preparatory Programs: Time for a Change." *Phi Delta Kappan* 62 no. 2 (October 1980): 120-122.

    Suggests some new admission criteria after arguing that present standards for admission to teacher education programs are generally inadequate to ensure that even a high-quality program will produce successful teachers.

250. Watts, Doyle. "Can Campus-Based Preservice Teacher Education Survive?" *Journal of Teacher Education* 33 no. 3 (May/June 1982): 48-52.

    Discusses six basic weaknesses in campus-based teacher education programs, including the problems of inadequate research and development activities and ineffective admissions standards.

251. Wheeler, Alan H. *Rhetoric to Reality: Implementing the Mandate for Excellence.* 1986. ERIC, ED 276 698.

    Outlines the need for more rigorous admission and exit criteria in programs for the preparation of teachers.

General Assessment of Progress

252. Adelman, Clifford, and others, eds. *Performance and Judgment: Essays on Principles and Practice in the Assessment of College Student Learning.* 1988. ERIC, ED 299 888.

    Outlines major technical issues concerning the assessment of student learning in higher education in light of sound principles and methods of testing and measurement.

253. Ashton, Patricia, and others. *Does Teacher Education Make a Difference? A Literature Review and Planning Study.* 1986. ERIC, ED 276 711.

Describes the evaluation of students' performance in preservice teacher education programs.

254. Bensen, Sterling O. "The Development of Teacher Competence: A Descriptive Study of Teachers' Perceptions of the Degree Prior Experiences, College Experiences, and Inservice Experiences Have Contributed to the Development of Forty-one Teacher Competencies." Ph.D. dissertation, University of Nebraska-Lincoln, 1977.

Investigates the perceived effect three separate stages in the lives of teachers had on the development of forty-one teaching competencies and provides an evaluation of the contributions that a teacher education program made toward this development.

255. Blake, Richard H. *Assessment of Inquiry Competencies in a Performance Based Teacher Education Program.* 1983. ERIC, ED 241 555.

Presents an assessment instrument that utilizes teacher and student behavioral objectives to determine the quality of instruction in a teacher education program.

256. Boser, Judith A., and others. *A Comparison of Participants in Traditional and Alternative Teacher Preparation Programs.* 1986. ERIC, ED 278 648.

Provides a comparison of the evaluation of students enrolled in traditional and alternative teacher preparation programs.

257. Brinkerhoff, Robert O. "Competency Assessment: A Perspective and an Approach." *Journal of Teacher Education* 29 no. 2 (1978): 21-24.

Examines the scope of competency assessment in teacher education programs and presents practical steps for organizing a structure for data gathering.

258. Denham, Carolyn. "Initiatives in Teacher Education in the
     California State System." *Action in Teacher Education.* 7 no. 1-2
     (Spring/Summer 1985): 41-44.

     Describes the evaluation of students in teacher education
     programs in the California State System.

259. Desaix, Margaret Lujean Swaim. "The Development and
     Implementation of an Objective-Independent Evaluation Model."
     Ph.D. dissertation, University of North Carolina at Chapel Hill,
     1978.

     Looks at the development and implementation of an objective-
     independent model which can be used in the evaluation of curricula
     where education objectives are absent.

260. Gollan, Ruth Nessel. "Students' Academic Ability and
     Perceptions of Various Aspects of College: Implications For
     Program Evaluation in Teacher Education." Ph.D. dissertation,
     Boston College, 1983.

     Explores whether groups of students with different ability levels
     (teacher education) vary in their satisfaction with the faculty, the
     administration, their major, and their fellow students.

261. Haddock, Marion David, Jr. "Course Assignments and Attitudes
     of Faculty and Students Toward Off-Campus Courses at Auburn
     University and Auburn University at Montgomery." Ed.D.
     dissertation, Auburn University, 1976.

     Studies faculty and students in the School of Education at
     Auburn University and Auburn University at Montgomery to
     determine differences in attitudes and course assignments in off-
     campus courses.

262. Hsu, Tse, and Shula F. Sadock. *Computer Assisted Test
     Construction: The State of the Art.* 1985. ERIC, ED 272 515.

     Provides an overview of current applications for computer
     technology to constructing list items and/or formulating tests
     according to sound measurement principles.

263. Hungerman, Ann D., and Carl F. Berger. *Longitudinal Assessment of Instructional Competency: Three Stages of Preservice Professional Development.* 1980. ERIC, ED 214 901.

    Reports the results of the implementation of a longitudinal evaluation system of students in the elementary teacher education programs at the University of Michigan.

264. Hurdle, Lois Stovall. "An Analysis of Predictor Variables of Student Achievement in General Education of Two Regional State Universities." Ph.D. dissertation, The University of Connecticut, 1980.

    Identifies variables that predict achievement in general education programs of two state universities.

265. Kalaian, Sima A., and Donald J. Freeman. *Relations Between Teacher Candidates' Self-Confidence and Orientations to Teaching.* 1987. ERIC, ED 300 366.

    Addresses the characteristics of students enrolled in teacher education programs relative to self-confidence and orientation to teaching.

266. Kozloff, Jessica. "A Student Centered Approach to Accountability and Assessment." *Journal of College Student Personnel* 28 no. 5 (September 1987): 419-424.

    Discusses ways by which current management perspective in assessing student outcomes can be redirected so that assessment is used primarily to promote student development and to enhance learning.

267. McDonald, Frederick J. "Evaluating Preservice Teachers' Competence." *Journal of Teacher Education* 29 no. 2 (1978): 9-13.

    Skills, knowledge, and attitudes of highly and moderately effective teachers are described and form the basis for the teacher education program and student evaluation.

268. McNergney, Robert and Martin Aylesworth. *Preservice Teacher Education Evaluation: An Overview.* 1983. ERIC, ED 236 167.

     Emphasizes the need for structured, ongoing evaluation of students as they pass through the various phases of a teacher education program.

269. Nelli, Elizabeth. "Five Myths in Need of Reality." *Action in Teacher Education* 3 no. 4 (Winter 1981/82): 1-6.

     Discusses the myths about teacher education students and describes some necessary evaluation systems.

270. Reighart, Penelope A., and William E. Loadman. *Content Analysis of Student Critical Events Reported in the Professional Introduction Courses.* 1984. ERIC, ED 248 202.

     Describes a system for analyzing the content of students' narrative reports of critical/significant events that occurred during experiences in introductory teacher education courses.

271. Renney, James E., and Victor L. Dupuis. *An Analysis of the Perceived Needs and Proficiencies of Preservice Teachers for Program Evaluation.* 1983. ERIC, ED 237 482.

     Compares the course content for prospective secondary teachers in two teacher education programs and provides comparisons of level of student achievement.

272. Riggs, Howard Norman. "A Descriptive Study of the Achievement of Elementary Education Students in Selected Methods Courses Conducted in a School/Campus Seating." Ph.D. dissertation, University of Minnesota, 1975.

     Looks at the achievement of elementary teacher education majors in methods courses taken in school settings with those taken on campus.

273. Rosario, Jose R., and Bette J. Soldwedel, eds. *Student Assessment in Teacher Education.* 1986. ERIC, ED 279 639.

     Describes a set of assessment tools to be used in the evaluation of students as they progress through a teacher education program.

274. Stiggins, Richard J. *Evaluating Students by Classroom Observation: Watching Students Grow.* 1984. ERIC, ED 243 941.

    Describes a guide to help teachers at all levels, including those in higher education, improve student assessments.

275. Stuck, Andrea F. "A Descriptive Study of the Cognitive and Psychosocial Development of Teacher Educators and Their Teacher Candidates." Ph.D. dissertation, The Ohio State University, 1984.

    Examines the cognitive and psychosocial development of teacher educators and teacher candidates in an entry level teacher education course.

276. Tanner, David E. *Teacher Education and Academic Rigor.* 1986. ERIC, ED 272 505.

    Investigates the various correlates of success by students in a teacher education program.

277. Taylor, Gerald D., and Peter J. Miller. "Professional Course Work and the Practicum: Do Good Students Make Good Teachers?" *Canadian Journal of Education* 10 no. 2 (Spring 1985): 105-120.

    Investigates the relationship between performance in professional course work and performance in the practicum in a professional year program for prospective elementary teachers.

278. Telfer, Karla Jean. "The Relationships Between the Professional Knowledge Component of the NTE Core Battery and Selected Variables of University Teacher Education Selective Retention Criteria." Ed.D. dissertation, Ball State University, 1985.

    Explores the relationships between scores from the NTE Core Battery and selected variables of Ball State University's secondary education selective retention program.

Laboratory Experiences

279. Alessia, Mary, and Kathleen Owens. *Handbook for Pre-Student Teaching Clinical Experiences. Secondary.* 1983. ERIC, ED 235 121.

Offers guidelines including evaluation materials, for the university supervisor, methods instructors, and cooperating teachers in providing a productive clinical experience for secondary teachers.

280. Altmann, Hal, and others. "Early Exploratory Field Experiences: An Effective Endeavor?" *Education Canada* 25 no. 2 (Summer 1985): 24-27.

Reports the results of a teacher education exploratory field experience evaluation project which indicated that students felt they benefited from early work in the field.

281. Applegate, Jane H. "Early Field Experiences: Three Viewpoints." In *Advances in Teacher Education, Volume 3*, edited by Martin Haberman and Julie M. Backus, 75-93. Norwood, NJ: Ablex Publishing Company, 1987.

Outlines some of the problems, issues, and ways of evaluating various types of early field experience programs.

282. Applegate, Jane H., and Thomas J. Lasley. "Students' Expectations for Early Field Experiences." *Texas Tech Journal of Education* 12 no. 1 (Winter 1985): 27-36.

Presents the expectations of teacher education students toward field experience programs and outlines the implications of the results for teacher education programs.

283. Arrozo, Aline Asa. "A Scale of Student Teaching Concerns For Use With Early Childhood Education Teacher Trainees." Ph.D. dissertation, Oregon State University, 1986.

Develops a Scale of Student Teaching Concerns to assess the concerns of early childhood teachers in training.

284. Atkinson, D. W., and L. T. Lavers. "Applied Studies: A Model for Experiential Education." *Alternative Higher Education: The Journal of Nontraditional Studies* 7 no. 1 (Fall/Winter 1982): 12-26.

    Describes an experiential educational model at the University of Lethbridge that allows for both employment and volunteer experiences, involves the awarding of academic credits, and places the onus on the student to document the relationship between field experiences and the academic program.

285. Augenstein, Patricia Alice Schram. "A Comparison of Student Teacher, Pupil and Regular Teacher Perceptions of Student Teacher Affect." Ph.D. dissertation, The University of Michigan, 1977.

    Determines if elementary student teachers possessed affective characteristics deemed desirable by professional educators and looks at the relationship among the ratings of teachers, the ratings of student teachers by pupils, and the self-ratings of student teachers.

286. Austin, Terri L., and Bob N. Cage. *Personality Influences on Student and Cooperating Teacher Attitudes Toward Teaching.* 1980. ERIC, ED 206 591.

    Reports the relationships between Jungian personality types of student and cooperating teachers to their attitudes and student teacher evaluations.

287. Bailey, Peter J. "Attributions, Affects, and Expectancies of Student Teachers." Ph.D. dissertation, University of Idaho, 1984.

    Examines the affective reactions and expectations for future performance within the context of student teaching.

288. Baker, Frederick J. "Alternative Sites for Student Teaching: A How-To-Do-It List for Successful Involvement." *Education* 104 no. 2 (Winter 1983): 184-187.

    Provides a "how-to-do-it" listing of activities for teacher education faculty to use prior to and during student teaching experiences in alternative sites.

289. Ball, Judith Irene. "The Effects on Student Teachers of Supervisory Personnel in an Innovative Student Teaching Experience." Ph.D. dissertation, University of Illinois at Urbana-Champaign, 1982.

　　　Examines the relationships of student teachers' levels of concern and their effects on student teaching practice without a cooperating teacher.

290. Barnes, Henrietta L. "The Conceptual Basis for Thematic Teacher Education Programs." *Journal of Teacher Education* 34 no. 8 (July/August 1987): 13-18.

　　　Provides a conceptual basis for the development and evaluation of a thematic teacher education program based on student teaching.

291. Barnes, Susan. *Student Teachers' Planning and Decision-Making Related to Pupil Evaluation.* 1983. ERIC, ED 240 104.

　　　Findings of an evaluation of the Clinical Teacher Education-Preservice Study were examined to determine the extent to which student teachers possessed planning and decision-making skills related to pupil evaluation.

292. Barrett, Joan. *Evaluation of Student Teachers. ERIC Digest 13.* 1986. ERIC, ED 278 658.

　　　Discusses the purpose of student teacher evaluation, criteria, measurement tools, evaluators, and elements of success.

293. Bergem, Trygve. "Teachers' Thinking and Behavior. An Empirical Study of the Role of Social Sensitivity and Moral Reasoning in the Teaching Performance of Student Teachers." *Scandinavian Journal of Educational Research* 30 no. 4 (1986): 193-203.

　　　Reports the results of a study of a moral component in teacher behavior, utilizing 14 different rating scales using supervising teachers as raters.

294. Berliner, David G. "Laboratory Settings and the Study of Teacher Education." *Journal of Teacher Education* 36 no. 6 (November/December 1985): 2-8.

Outlines the use of the research base in teacher education and advocates that pedagogy must become a laboratory-based field study, with environments in which to experiment with producing cognitive and affective changes in children.

295. Bishop, Laurence Allan. "Student Teaching Effectiveness as a Function of the Personalities of Supervising Teachers and Student Teachers." Ph.D. dissertation, University of California, Berkeley, 1975.

Analyzes the correlates of the personalities of elementary supervising teachers and the classroom performances of their student teachers.

296. Blackmon, C. Robert, and others. *Evaluation of Student Teachers: Ratings by Supervising Teachers on Nine Performance Variables.* 1978. ERIC, ED 164 489.

Presents the results of a two year study of the ratings given by supervising teachers to student teachers along with nine performance variables considered important to student teaching including enthusiasm, English usage, poise, classroom control, teaching skills, organization, command of subject, general information, and overall teaching performance.

297. Blair, Timothy R. *The Relationship Between Reading Methods Courses and Student Teaching.* 1982. ERIC, ED 215 293.

Outlines the results of a study designed to compare the performances of undergraduates on a knowledge test of reading administered before and after student teaching with the amount of effort committed to reading instruction by their respective supervisory teachers.

298. Blanton, Linda P., and Michael J. Fimian. "Perceptions of
     Special Education Teacher Trainee Competence." *Teacher
     Education and Special Education* 9 no. 3 (Summer 1986): 113-
     122.

     Analyzes teacher trainee performance ratings collected from
     special education teacher trainees, university supervisors, and
     cooperating teachers and reveals that all three groups perceived
     identical factor--instructional management, cognitive strategies
     instruction, and career/vocational education--as underlying the
     construct of teacher trainee competence.

299. Bontempo, Barbara T., and others. "Helping Cooperating Teacher
     of Early Field Experiences." *Teacher Education Quarterly* 13 no. 1
     (Winter 1986): 72-81.

     Discusses four phases of a plan and guidelines to help
     cooperating teachers monitor early field experience programs for the
     preparation of teachers.

300. Booker, John M. and Richard E. Riedl. "Evaluating the
     Performance of a Rural, Field-Based Teacher Training Program."
     Research in Rural Education 4 no. 2 (Spring 1987): 47-51.

     Findings from the study indicated most successful students in
     the University of Alaska-Fairbanks rural field-based teacher
     education program over a three-year period show poorer
     performance when conventional standards for course completion are
     applied.

301. Botsford, Michael Locke. "Assessing the Effectiveness of a Field-
     Centered Performance-Based Teacher Education Program." Ed.D.
     dissertation, University of Southern California, 1975.

     Identifies the strengths and weaknesses in a field-centered
     performance-based teacher education program.

302. Boyan, Norman J., and Willis D. Copeland. *Instructional Supervision Training Program.* Columbus, OH: Charles E. Merrill Publishing Co., 1978.

    Outlines an extensive system of instructional supervision and instrumentation for the evaluation of student teaching and other types of classroom experiences.

303. Brothers, Linda Ruth Friesner. "The Relationship Between Field Experiences and Teacher Trainees' Self-Concept and Attitude." Ph.D. dissertation, Purdue University, 1984.

    Reviews the relationships between field experiences, self-concept, attitude toward teaching, and the perceived impact of the field experiences.

304. Brown, Ric. *The Training of Teachers Using Observations of BTES Variables.* 1979. ERIC, ED 196 900.

    Describes a study of student teachers, in which the results of the Beginning Teacher Evaluation Study were infused into the classroom.

305. Brown, William R. "Checklist for Assessment of Science Teachers and Its Use in a Science Preservice Teacher Education Project." *Journal of Research in Science Teaching* 10 no. 3 (1973): 243-249.

    Outlines the development and validation of an instrument to be used in observing student teachers in the classroom.

306. Calfee, Timothy Hogan. "The Relationship Between Early Field Experience and Performance During Student Teaching." Ph.D. dissertation, The University of Akron, 1983.

    Discusses the relationship between early field experience and performance during student teaching.

307. Callahan, Richard Charles. "The Effects of Student Teaching and Pupil Evaluation on Attitudes of Student Teachers." Ph.D. dissertation, University of Oregon, 1976.

Describes the attitudes of student teachers at the outset and conclusion of student teaching and measures the effects of pupil feedback on attitudes.

308. Cannon, Haskell D., and others. *Program for Learning Competent Teaching.* 1986. ERIC, ED 288 841.

Describes an on-site preservice teacher training program that is conducted in the public schools that includes academic content courses, methods content, teaching skills, and personal development work.

309. Capie, William, and others. *Using Pupil Achievement to Validate Ratings of Student Teacher Performance.* 1980. ERIC, ED 191 916.

Reports the magnitude of simple and multiple correlations between the Teacher Performance Assessment Instruments (TPAI) ratings of elementary student teachers and achievement gains of their pupils and certain methodological and contextual factors on the validity coefficients generated.

310. Caplin, Morris, D. *Evaluating Student Teaching.* 1980. ERIC, ED 191 800.

Reports the results of a Queens College Study which indicates that practicing teachers are more interested in better and earlier screening of potential teachers, more applicable teacher education courses, and the ability of a cooperating teacher to add the responsibility of supervising a student teacher to an already heavy load.

311. Chicago, University of Illinois at. *Teaching in the Secondary Schools: A Guide for Pre-Service Teachers.* 1987. ERIC, ED 298 098.

Presents a guidebook for preservice secondary student teachers which outlines in detail the techniques for relating field experiences to the academic work in the university classroom and ways of evaluating the work in field experiences.

312. Coker, Joan G. "A Study of Student Teaching Using Direct Observation." Ed.D. dissertation, Georgia State University, 1978.

Explores the use of the Classroom Observation Keyed to Effectiveness Research instrument in the evaluation of student teachers and utilizes the instrument to compare three groups of student teachers at different institutions.

313. Corbett, Henry Dickson, III. "Which Others: A Study of Determinants of Influential Others for Student Teachers." Ph.D. dissertation, University of North Carolina at Chapel Hill, 1978.

Addresses the question of who influences student teachers in their development as teachers.

314. Cox, C. Benjamin, and others. *A Study of the Effects of Pairing Social Studies Student Teachers.* 1981. ERIC, ED 222 429.

Outlines the results of an experimental study in which pairs of student teachers were assigned to one cooperating teacher, with the results indicating that cooperating and student teachers approach teaching as a craft and that student teachers see a stronger connection between their subject matter courses and student teaching than between their professional courses and student teaching.

315. Cronin, Janice Tilleros. "A Study of the Attitudes of Selected Groups Toward the Student Teaching Program at the University of Iowa." Ph.D. dissertation, The University of Iowa, 1986.

Explores the key concepts and roles perceived by student teachers, cooperating teachers, college supervisors, and building administrators.

316. Curwin, Richard L., and Barbara Schneider Fuhrmann. *Discovering Your Teaching Self: Humanistic Approaches to Effective Teaching.* Englewood Cliffs, NJ: Prentice-Hall, 1975.

Includes a compilation of worksheets, inventories, vignettes, self-awareness inventories, questions of analysis, and diagrams to

help understand the instructional process and the technical
competencies needed in the classroom during student teaching.

317. Davis, Brian K. *Field Experience: What is It? Why is It Out
     There?* 1982. ERIC, ED 222 447.

     Examines the role of field experiences in the teacher education
     curriculum and suggests ways of evaluating these experiences and
     incorporating the results into the preservice programs for the
     preparation of teachers.

318. Davis, James, and others. "A Study of the Internship Experience."
     Journal of Experiential Learning 10 no. 2 (Summer 1987): 22-24.

     Results of a three year study of over 200 student interns in
     teacher education indicated the participants felt internships helped
     them locate jobs, test career interests, provide opportunities to
     integrate classroom learning with field experience, and better
     understand personal and career goals.

319. Dawson, Jack Leslie. "Clinical and Nonclinical Supervision of
     Student Teachers." Ph.D. dissertation, University of Idaho, 1982.

     Outlines evaluation procedures to determine the outcomes of the
     clinical supervision process with student teachers.

320. DeBruin, Jerome E. *A Developmental Perspective on the Growth
     of Student Teachers Using the COKER and TPAI.* 1983. ERIC,
     ED 228 223.

     Reports the results of the use of two student teacher evaluation
     methods including the Classroom Observation Keyed to
     Effectiveness Research Instrument and the Teacher Performance
     Assessment Instrument.

321. Defino, Maria E. *The Evaluation of Student Teachers.* 1983.
     ERIC, ED 240 103.

     Presents a review of pertinent literature on the evaluation of
     student teachers, including descriptions of differing evaluation
     approaches and techniques, and descriptions of various types of data
     analysis and interpretations of results.

322. deLaski-Smith, Deb, and Joy Hansen. "A New Approach to Field Experience." *Journal of Home Economics* 75 no. 1 (Spring 1983): 38-44.

    Provides a detailed description of a field experience course for home economics, including course development, organization, and administration, field placement, evaluation, and the pre-enrollment workshop.

323. Denton, Jon J., and Ebrahim Kazimi. *Relations Among Final Supervisor Skill Ratings of Student Teachers and Cognitive Attainment Values of Learners Taught by Student Teachers.* 1982. ERIC, ED 212 589.

    Concludes that developing lesson plans, using different levels of classroom questions, performance while student teaching two-week units, and personal energy are related to pupil achievement.

324. Denton, John J., and Lorna J. Lacina. *Quantity of Professional Education Coursework Linked with Process Measures of Student Teaching.* 1982. ERIC, ED 219 355.

    Reports a study to determine differences between supervisors' ratings of the instructional competencies of education majors and non-education majors in a semester of student teaching and also includes evaluations by education majors and non-education majors of their morale during a student teaching program.

325. Denton, Jon J., and Sherrill A. Norris. *Cognitive Attainment of Learners of Student Teachers: A Criterion for Attaining Accountable Teacher Preparation Programs.* 1979. ERIC, ED 178 516.

    Employs learner cognitive attainment as a measure of student teacher effectiveness; five conceptual reasearch models are used to determine the teaching skill level of student teachers.

326. Dickson, George E., and others. *A Comparison of Teaching Performance as Measured through Observation of Student Teachers and Experienced Teachers.* 1984. ERIC, ED 244 935.

    Shows a comparison between 20 experienced teachers and 336 student teachers as measured by use of the Classroom Observation

Keyed for Effectiveness Research Instrument and the Teacher
Performance Assessment Instrument.

327. Donofrio, Angela M., and others. *Age and Experience as Factors
Affecting Student Attitudes Toward Experience-Based Teacher
Training Programs.* 1980. ERIC, ED 182 309.

Reports the results of a study to determine the attitudes of
undergraduate education students regarding the importance of
experiences with children and to examine the effects of age, prior
experiences with children, and class standing on their attitudes.

328. Duffy, Pat. "Student Perceptions of Tutor Expectations for
School-Based Teaching Practice." *European Journal of Teacher
Education* 10 no. 3 (1987).

Summarizes an examination of education majors' perceptions of
their supervisors' expectations regarding their performances as
student teachers.

329. D'Zmura, Justine Rusnock. "The Effect of a Specially Designed
Course in *Classroom Management: Theory and Techniques* on the
Learnings, Attitudes, and Performance of Student Teachers in Their
Supervised Practica." Ph.D. dissertation, Bryn Mawr College,
1976.

Investigates the effects of a specially designed course in
classroom management on the learning, attitudes, and performance
of elementary student teachers in their supervised practica.

330. Edwards, Sara A. *Clinical Preservice Activities: Education,
Development, Training--Three Case Studies. Clinical Teacher
Education--Preservice Series.* 1982. ERIC, ED 240 099.

Reports three findings from a major study: (1) the lack of an
articulated, agreed-upon knowledge base regarding the content and
process of either teaching or preparing the student teacher; (2)
personal characteristics of the members of the student teaching triad
are highly predictive of the interactions and evaluations which take
place in the clinical experience; and (3) craft knowledge and
"common sense" are the basis of most on-the-scene decisions
regarding specific experiences and behaviors.

331. Elliott, Peggy G. "A Study of the Influence of the Amount of Previous University Directed Field Experience, Length of Assignment, and Number of Classroom Supervisors on Secondary Student Teachers Perceived Impact on Pupil Instruction." Ed.D. dissertation, Indiana University, 1975.

   Investigates differences in perceptions of secondary student teachers as to how some aspects of their experiences related to their impact on pupil instruction.

332. Elsworth, Gerald B., and Frank Coulter. *Aspiration and Attainment: The Measurement of Professional Self Perception in Student Teachers.* 1977. ERIC, ED 198 169.

   Reports the development and field testing of a semantic differential designed to measure professional self perception in student teachers.

333. Fagan, Edward R., and others. *Secondary Teacher Education. A Model for the Eighties.* 1981. ERIC, ED 212 616.

   Includes a series of papers dealing with such contemporary issues as theoretical models for teacher education program change, an analysis of the five stages in the development of novice teachers, the evaluation of field experiences, and internal evaluations of reformulated programs.

334. Fargo, J. Steven. "Evaluation of Two Teacher Preparation Programs at Northern Arizona University as Measured by Student Teaching Performance and Attitude." Ed.D. dissertation, Northern Arizona University, 1988.

   Compares two different approaches for the preparation of teachers.

335. Flaquer-Gonzalez, Nydia Maria. "The Perceived Roles of Secondary Student Teachers and Cooperating Teachers as Related to the Satisfaction and Effectiveness of Student Teachers." Ed.D. dissertation, New York University, 1987.

   Investigates the relationship between the perceptions of roles and the satisfaction and effectiveness of student teachers.

336. Flint, Deborah Anne. "The Relationship Between Classroom
     Experience and the Anxiety of Practice Teachers Beginning an
     Intensive Period of Student Teaching." Ph.D. dissertation,
     University of Southern California, 1983.

     Investigates whether a gradual introduction to student teaching
     was related to trainees' anxiety regarding student teaching.

337. Folkert, Lynn A. "A Study of the Relationship Between Early
     Field Experience and Student Teaching Performance at the
     Secondary Level." Ph.D. dissertation, Michigan State University,
     1977.

     Looks at the relationship between early field experience and
     student teaching performance at the secondary level.

338. Foster, Phillip R., and others. *Assessment of Industrial Arts Field
     Experiences.* 1985. ERIC, ED 266 255.

     Outlines a project to assess and improve existing field
     experience programs for future industrial arts teachers; includes
     evaluation indicators of success for the program.

339. Fredericks, Terence Duncan. "The Concerns of Graduate Student
     Teachers: A Developmental Conceptualization." Ed.D.
     dissertation, Columbia University Teachers College, 1986.

     Identifies and examines the concerns of graduate student teachers
     during student teaching in comparison with undergraduate student
     teachers.

340. Freed, Harvey Franklin. "Role Expectations of the College
     Supervisor of Student Teaching as Perceived by Supervisors,
     Principals, Cooperating Teachers, and Student Teachers." Ed.D.
     dissertation, Temple University, 1976.

     Investigates the role expectations of the college supervisor of
     student teaching as seen by supervisors, principals, cooperating
     teachers, and student teachers.

341. Freiberg, H. Jerome, and others. *Improving the Quality of Student Teaching.* 1987. ERIC, ED 288 233.

   Describes the results of an experiment to help evaluate student teachers in which subjects were assigned to one of three groups: the control group received ordinary supervisor feedback, the "experimental feedback" group received feedback from a classroom analysis scheme--the Stallings Observation System (SOS), and the "experimental seminar" group also received feedback from the SOS, but with guidance and discussion on how to use it for self-improvement.

342. Freiberg, H. Jerome, and Hersholt C. Waxman. "Alternative Feedback Approaches to Improving Student Teachers' Classroom Instruction." *Journal of Teacher Education* 39 no. 4 (July/August 1988): 8-14.

   Describes three approaches for providing feedback for improving classroom instruction of preservice teachers: (1) feedback from pupils; (2) feedback from classroom observation; and (3) self-analysis of classroom lessons.

343. Friebus, Robert J. "Agents of Socialization Involved in Student Teaching." *Journal of Educational Research* 70 no. 5 (May/June 1977): 263-268.

   Identifies the agents who are responsible for the socialization of student teachers in the schools, and provides suggestions for evaluating the process.

344. Funk, Fanchon F., and others. *An Instrument for Use by Supervising Teachers in Evaluating Student Teaching Programs.* 1981. ERIC, ED 201 624.

   Outlines the development and utilization of a questionnaire designed to gather feedback information from cooperating teachers on the strengths and weaknesses of teacher education programs.

345. Funk, Fanchon F., and others. *The Influence of Feedback from Supervising Teachers on a Student Teaching Program.* 1978. ERIC, ED 211 492.

    Describes the Supervising Teacher's Evaluation Form and the results of its use to gather information from supervising teachers on the adequacy of the student teacher's training, the adequacy of the university supervisor's supervision of student teachers, and the adequacy of the Office of Field Experiences in the duties of supervision, cooperation, and communication with supervising teachers

346. Funk, Fanchon F., and others. "Student Teaching Program: Feedback from Supervising Teachers." *Clearing House* 55 no. 7 (March 1982): 319-321.

    Provides an example of a comprehensive form for obtaining specific evaluative data related to teacher education programs and reports on the findings of preliminary investigations using the form.

347. Gallaher, Thomas H., and others. "A Three Role Group Clinical Supervision System for Student Teaching." *Journal of Teacher Education* 34 no. 2 (March/April 1983): 48-51.

    Describes the results and evaluation of the use of a clinical supervision system with three role group--student teaching teams, university supervisors, and cooperating teachers.

348. Gallemore, Sandra L. *Student Teaching Objectives: Their Importance and Achievement.* 1979. ERIC, ED 218 265.

    Outlines the results of a study to determine the value of student teaching by examining the attitudes of student teachers, cooperating teachers, and university supervisors toward the objectives and skills to be achieved during student teaching.

349. Garman, Noreen B. "Reflection, the Heart of Clinical Supervision: A Modern Rationale for Professional Practice." *Journal of Curriculum and Supervision* 2 no. 1 (Fall 1986): 1-24.

    Traces the roots of clinical supervision for teacher-scholars, explicates a professional knowledge base, examines reflection as a primary inquiry process, provides scenarios for teaching and supervisor-teacher collaboration, outlines a system for evaluation, and includes extensive references.

350. Gaskell, Peter James. "Patterns and Change in the Perspectives of Student Teachers: A Participant Observation Study." Ed.D. dissertation, Harvard University, 1975.

   Investigates the development of common perspectives among student teachers and the links to program variables.

351. Georgia State Department of Education. *Professional Laboratory Experiences in Georgia Teacher Education.* 1980. ERIC, ED 210 272.

   Provides an outline of the policies, procedures, responsibilities, evaluation procedures, and functions of Georgia agencies and individuals participating in laboratory experiences for teacher education students.

352. Gibney, Thomas, and William Wiersma. "Using Profile Analysis for Student Teacher Evaluation." *Journal of Teacher Education* 37 no. 3 (May/June 1986): 41-45.

   Outlines an assessment system of the performance of student teachers utilizing two approaches to observation which use established observation inventories.

353. Gitlin, Andrew, and others. *Horizontal Evaluation: An Investigation Into an Approach to Student Teacher Supervision.* 1982. ERIC, ED 214 904.

   Reports a study to determine the effectiveness of horizontal evaluation for student teachers and their supervisors through the use of qualitative analysis of three case studies.

354. Glasgow, Dorothy D. "Perceptions of Student Teachers, Supervising Teachers, and Professors of Education Toward Selected Issues in Student Teaching." Ed.D. dissertation, Florida Atlantic University, 1986.

Outlines the perceptions of student teachers, supervising teachers, and professors of education toward selected issues in student teaching.

355. Griffin, Gary A., and Sara Edwards, eds. *Student Teaching: Problems and Promising Practices.* 1982. ERIC, ED 223 571.

Examines a variety of issues related to all aspects of student teaching, including laboratory experiences, evaluation, and assessment.

356. Griffin, Gary A., and others. *Clinical Preservice Teacher Education.* 1983. ERIC, ED 240 100.

Presents a final report of a major multi-site, multi-method investigation of student teaching, including detailed information on the evaluation methods that are used in student teaching programs.

357. Grossman, George C. *A Comparison of the Effectiveness of Student Teachers Who Have Had Extensive Early Field Experience With Those Who Have Not.* 1980. ERIC, ED 207 943.

Outlines the development, implementation, and evaluation of an early field experience program and makes comparisons with students who have completed the early program prior to student teaching with those who did not have the experiences.

358. Hadley, Marilyn Bowen. "A Study to Validate Selected Student Teaching Competencies in the Upper Midwest." Ed.D. dissertation, University of South Dakota, 1976.

Reports the validation of selected student teacher competencies in the Upper Midwest.

359. Haggard, Cynthia S. "Differentiated Student Teacher Evaluations: Weighted Variables." Ed.D. dissertation, Indiana University, 1986.

    Investigates whether using weighted descriptors to evaluate student teachers results in a differentiated evaluation profile.

360. Harris, Paulette Proctor. "An Investigation of Preservice Teachers' Verbal Behaviors During Field Experience Lesson Presentation." Ed.D. dissertation, University of South Carolina, 1983.

    Measures and describes any alterations of preservice teachers' verbal behaviors and related skills that occur during teacher education training.

361. Hattie, John, and others. "Assessment of Student Teachers by Supervising Teachers." *Journal of Educational Psychology* 74 no. 5 (October 1982): 778-785.

    Reports that supervising teachers appear to reliably evaluate student teachers and tend to perceive student teachers in terms of two major factors--preparation and presentation.

362. Hawdyshell, Judy Ann Bussard. "Some Effects of Microteaching, Cooperating Teachers, University Supervisors, and Discussion Style Upon Classroom Teaching During Student Teaching." Ed.D. dissertation, University of Illinois at Urbana-Champaign, 1986.

    Examines the assumption that after training is completed, microteaching is an effective method of increasing the range of behaviors employed by teachers in the classroom.

363. Hawkins, Andrew H., and others. *Teaching Performance of Undergraduate Physical Education Majors across Teacher Education Program Practica.* 1986. ERIC, ED 273 594.

    Outlines the results of a study of the establishment of a descriptive base for the performances of physical education preservice teachers as they progress through various types of practica experiences leading to student teaching.

364. Haysom, John. *Inquiring into the Teaching Process: Towards Self Evaluation and Professional Development.* Toronto: The Ontario Institute for Studies in Education, 1985.

Provides a series of activities for examining the life in the classroom, including classroom observation, perceptual guides, sociograms, and other inventories that can be used in learning about student teachers.

365. Heath, Marie Pearl. "An Examination of the Curriculum of Early Field Experiences in Selected Teacher Education Programs in Ohio." Ph.D. dissertation, The Ohio State University, 1984.

Describes some pre-student teaching field experiences in Ohio, the context in which they are provided, and the variables of the different institutions which provide them.

366. Henry, Marvin. "The Effect of Increased Exploratory Field Experiences upon the Perceptions and Performance of Student Teachers." *Action in Teacher Education* 5 no. 1-2 (Spring/Summer 1983): 66-70.

Reports the effects of increased field experiences on the perceptions and performances of 238 secondary school student teachers and concludes that an increased number of required field experiences had little impact on student teachers' evaluations of their teaching ability or on supervising teachers' final evaluations of student teachers' performances.

367. Hensley, Robert Byron. "Student Teachers' Perceptions of the Utility of Undergraduate Elementary Education Courses." Ph.D. dissertation, Texas A & M University, 1986.

Examines undergraduate elementary education majors' perceptions of their professional preparation courses.

368. Hoffman, Roy A., and Murray I. Gellen. "A Comparison of Self-evaluations and Classroom Teacher Evaluations for Aides in a Pre-student Teaching Field Experience Program." *Teacher Educator* 17 no. 2 (Fall 1981): 16-21.

Outlines a study of preservice students who evaluated their performance as student aides and found that female aides in elementary classroom settings evaluated their performance to be significantly less satisfactory than did their cooperating teachers.

369. Holloway, Elizabeth L. "Characteristics of the Field Practicum: A National Survey." *Counselor Education and Supervision* 22 no. 1 (September 1982): 75-80.

Reports the results of a national survey of current and ideal characteristics of practicum activities, trainee evaluation, and supervisory requirements from 287 counselor education programs.

370. Holly, Mary Louise. *Keeping a Personal-Professional Journal.* Victoria, Australia: Deakin University, 1984.

Provides guidance on keeping a journal reflecting upon events and occurrences in classroom practice.

371. Hopkins, David. *A Teacher's Guide to Classroom Research.* Stony Stratford, England: Open University Press, 1985.

Provides a description of classroom action research by teachers which may be of value in evaluating teacher education programs involving field experiences.

372. Hopsan, Theresa M. Garrett. "Supervising Teachers' and Student Teachers' Perceptions of the Actual and Ideal Role of the Elementary Supervising Teacher." Ph.D. dissertation, The University of Michigan, 1981.

Defines and describes the actual and ideal role of the supervising teacher as perceived by the cooperating teacher and student teacher in elementary education.

373. Howey, Kenneth R., and Nancy L. Zimpher. *Profiles of Preservice Teacher Education: Inquiry into the Nature of Programs.* Albany, NY: SUNY Press, 1989.

Summarizes a detailed study of the preservice teacher education programs of a group of mid-west teacher programs, including the field experience components.

374. Ihedigbo, Apollos Ndulaka. "A Survey of the Role Expectations of the Supervision of Student Teachers." Ed.D. dissertation, University of Massachusetts, 1987.

   Examines the role expectations of the university supervisors of student teachers during student teaching field experiences.

375. Irvine, Jacqueline Jordan. "The Accuracy of Pre-Service Teachers' Assessments of Their Classroom Behaviors." *Journal of Research and Development in Education* 17 no. 1 (Fall 1983): 25-31.

   Reports an investigation of the concurrence between preservice teachers' self-evaluations and the ratings of their supervisors after student teachers and supervisors completed training designed to facilitate self-assessment and collegiate relationships.

376. Irvine, Jacqueline Jordan. *The Effects of the Integrated Model for the Training and Supervision of Teachers on the Self-Assessment Skills of Pre-Service Teachers.* 1982. ERIC, ED 215 963.

   Describes the Integrated Model for the Training and Supervision of Teachers (IMTS), a systems approach with a delineated sequence of seven clinical supervision phases integrated with performance-based criteria for self and supervision assessment.

377. Jacobson, Phyllis Lynne. "Student Teachers' Use of Evaluation Information." Ed.D. dissertation, University of California, Los Angeles, 1989.

   Investigates the context, source, and type of evaluation information provided to student teachers and the use made of it.

378. James, Terry L., and Wayne Dumas. "College GPA as a Predictor of Teacher Competency: A New Look at an Old Question." *Journal of Experimental Education* 44 no. 4 (Summer 1976): 40-43.

   Reports the results of a study to relate grade point average to success in student teaching.

379. Johnson, Jim, and John Yates. *A National Survey of Student Teaching Programs.* 1982. ERIC, ED 232 963.

Findings are presented of research on 902 student teaching programs divided into three areas including administration of student teaching programs, selected aspects regarding the student teachers themselves and ways of conducting evaluations, and selected aspects of cooperating teachers and school districts.

380. Johnson, Lawrence J. "Factors that Influence Skill Acquisition of Practicum Students during a Field-Based Experience." *Teacher Education and Special Education* 9 no. 3 (Summer 1986): 89-103.

Reports the results of a study of the influence on practicum students' acquisition of teaching skills for mainstreaming handicapped children in which it was revealed that cooperating teachers, university supervisors, course work, field experiences, and practicum assignments exerted the greatest influence on student teachers.

381. Johnson, Lawrence J., Jr. "Factors That Influence Skill Acquisition of Practicum Students During a Field-Based Experience." Ph.D. dissertation, University of Illinois at Urbana-Champaign, 1985.

Reviews the influences of individuals and/or events on practicum students' acquisition of selected teaching skills.

382. Johnson, Mary Lynn. *Cognitive Attainment of Learners of Student Teachers Across Two Units of Study.* 1982. ERIC, ED 221 525.

Reports the results of a study of student teachers to determine the relationship between cognitive attainment of learners across two units of study.

383. Kagan, Dona M. "The Heuristic Value of Regarding Classroom Instruction as an Aesthetic Medium." *Educational Researcher* 18 no. 6 (August/September 1989): 11-18.

Outlines an approach to the evaluation of teachers that defines classroom instruction as an aesthetic medium in which a lesson can be evaluated alternatively as a kinetic performance, a message, and a work of art.

384. Kahre, Charleen Joan. "Relationships Between Learning Styles of Student Teachers, Cooperating Teachers, and Final Evaluations." Ph.D. dissertation, Arizona State University, 1984.

   Describes the relationships between learning style of preferences of student teachers and their cooperating teachers and its effect on the student teachers' final evaluation.

385. Kilgore, Alvah M. *Implementing Educational Equity Practices in a Field-Based Teacher Education Program: Some Promising Practices.* 1982. ERIC, ED 214 919.

   Reports an extensive evaluation design for field-based teacher education programs with particular emphasis on student teaching.

386. Killian, Joyce E., and D. John McIntyre. "Quality in the Early Field Experiences: A Product of Grade Level and Cooperating Teachers' Training." *Teaching and Teacher Education* 2 no. 4 (1986): 367-376.

   Discusses the evaluation and results of a study designed to examine the effect of a cooperating teacher trained in supervision of preservice teachers as well as the effect of grade level assigned on the quality of early field experiences.

387. Kingen, Sharon. "Does the Left Hand Really Know What the Right Hand is Doing? An Informal Look at the Selection and Evaluation of Cooperating Teachers." *Teacher Educator* 20 no. 1 (Summer 1984): 2-13.

   Explores criteria for selecting and evaluating the cooperating teacher.

388. Kitchens, Roger Hilliard. "An Early Field-Experience Program in Teacher Education: A Grounded Theory Study." Ed.D. dissertation, Arizona State University, 1983.

   Uses methodology of grounded theory to examine an early field-experience teacher education program at Arizona State University.

389. Konefal, Janet. "A Case Study Analysis of the Relationship Between A University Supervisor and Student Teachers." Ph.D. dissertation, University of Miami, 1981.

     Studies the role of a University supervisor as it relates to the needs and problems of a specific group of student teachers.

390. Kuehl, Raymond. *A Taxonomy of Critical Tasks for Evaluating Student Teaching.* 1979. ERIC, ED 179 544.

     Reports the results of a study to develop a taxonomy of critical tasks that are necessary for evaluating the effectiveness of student teaching as perceived by cooperating teachers, student teachers, school administrators, and college teacher educators.

391. Lamb, Charles E., and Earl J. Montague. *Variables Pertaining to the Perceived Effectiveness of University Student Teaching Supervisors.* 1982. ERIC, ED 212 613.

     Reports the results of a study in which student teachers and cooperating teachers rated the effectiveness and performance of university supervisors in the student teaching process.

392. Lawson, Marlene Ola Tyler. "The Relationship Between Ratings of Student Competencies as Defined by Methods Course Objectives and of Performance in Student Teaching in a Teacher Education Program." Ed.D. dissertation, The George Washington University, 1983.

     Reports student performance in a block methods course as an indicator of performance in student teaching.

393. Lester, Paula E. *Teacher Job Satisfaction.* New York: Garland Publishing, 1988.

     Includes over 1,000 annotated references to teacher job satisfaction that may be useful in evaluating the laboratory experiences program in teacher education.

394. Lourie, Nancy E. *An Analysis of a College Supervisory Position in Teacher Education from an Organizational Perspective.* 1982. ERIC, ED 215 959.

    Reports an analysis and reorganization of a student teacher program and an exploratory study of the roles and responsibilities of college supervisors from an organizational perspective.

395. Luttrell, H. Dale, and others. *Paid Early Field Experience for College Education Majors.* 1982. ERIC, ED 214 934.

    Outlines the results of a study in which preservice teacher education students participated in a program in which they received pay for working in the schools as aides and in other capacities and also received academic credit toward their degrees.

396. MacNaugton, Robert H., and others. "Getting It Together." *Peabody Journal of Education* 55 no. 2 (1978): 82-89.

    Describes a student teaching evaluation instrument designed to reinforce instructional and supervisory models acquired during preservice education and to provide a bridge between university methods instruction and student teaching.

397. Mahan, James M., and Jerome C. Harste. *Professional Judgment as a Criterion Variable in Pre-service Teacher Education Research.* 1977. ERIC, ED 135 761.

    Reports the results of a three-year study in which professional judgment was used as a criterion variable in the evaluation of student teachers.

398. Malone, Mark R., and Barbara M. Strawitz. *Relative Effects of Microteaching and Field Experience on Preservice Teachers.* 1985. ERIC, ED 297 962.

    Presents the results of a study designed to determine whether preservice elementary teachers with a great deal of previous early field experience, but not previous microteaching experience, would benefit more from an additional science field experience in the local school system or from an alternative science microteaching experience.

399. McBraver, Daniel J., and Ronald E. Williamson. *Field Experience Evaluation: A Paradigm for Preservice Practica.* 1986. ERIC, ED 275 672.

    Describes an evaluation method which may be used as a tool in the comprehensive evaluation of preservice teacher education field experience programs.

400. McIntyre, D. John. *Field Experiences in Teacher Education: From Student to Teacher.* 1983. ERIC, ED 225 942.

    Provides a comprehensive analysis of the literature on field experiences for preservice teachers divided into five sections including influences of field experiences on the attitudes and behavior of preservice teachers, roles of university student teacher supervisors and cooperating teachers, structure of field experience program and models, evaluation of student teacher performance during field experiences, and assessment of the success of field experiences.

401. McIntyre, D. John, and Tom Rusk Vickery. *Differential Observer Effects on Student Teachers.* 1980. ERIC, ED 198 071.

    Reports a study testing the hypothesis that cooperating teachers and student teacher supervisors, as observers, affect the student teachers' verbal behavior differently.

402. Mears, Ruth Anne. "Student Teacher/Cooperating Teacher Relationships, Perceptions of Conferences, and Student Morale." Ph.D. dissertation, The Pennsylvania State University, 1981.

    Reviews the relationships between student teachers and their supervisors.

403. Medrano, Hilda H. "Effects of Classroom Management Training on Selected Teaching Behaviors of Student Teachers." Ph.D. dissertation, The University of Texas at Austin, 1985.

    Assesses the extent to which elementary student teachers can implement research-derived classroom management strategies.

404. Michael, Robert O., and others. *Using Field-Based Experiences as a Guide for Program Evaluation and Redesign.* 1987. ERIC, ED 287 220.

   Utilizing the results of the evaluation of field experience programs, one institution redesigned programs for the preparation of educational administrators.

405. Minehart, Charlotte Heasley. "An Ethnography of Evolving Student Teacher Concerns." Ed.D. dissertation, West Virginia University, 1985.

   Utilized ethnographic methodology to examine the evolving concerns of student teachers.

406. Morris, John E. *Student Teacher Performance in an Eight Weeks and a Full Semester Program: Perceptions of Supervising Teachers.* 1980. ERIC, ED 195 538.

   Describes a comparative analysis of an eight week and a full semester program in student teaching based in part on the perceptions of supervising teachers.

407. Morris, June Rose. "The Effects of the University Supervisor on the Performance and Adjustment of Student Teachers." *Journal of Educational Research* 67 no. 8 (April 1974): 358-362.

   Reports the results of a study to determine the effects of the university supervisor on the performance and adjustment of student teachers.

408. Morris, Stephen B., and Leonard J. Haas. "Evaluating Undergraduate Field Placements: An Empirical Approach." *Teaching of Psychology* 11 no. 3 (October 1984): 166-168.

   Reports a method for evaluating undergraduate field experiences in psychology that takes into account attainment of individual goals and quality of supervision.

409. Morrow, John E., and John M.Lane. "Instructional Problems of Student Teachers: Perceptions of Student Teachers, Supervising Teachers and College Supervisors." *Action in Teacher Education* 5 no. 1-2 (Spring/Summer 1983): 71-78.

Compares student teachers', supervising teachers', and college supervisors' perceptions regarding the instructional problems of student teachers and concludes the findings are consistent with past research in the same area.

410. Nelson, David, and Wesley Sandness. *Self-Evalution in Student Teaching: A Reanalysis.* 1986. ERIC, ED 288 843.

Examines how grade level and gender affect student teachers' self-ratings and faculty and field supervisors' ratings of student teachers' performance.

411. Network, The, Inc. *A Compendium of Innovative Teacher Education Projects.* Andover, MA: The Network, Inc., 1987.

Includes a compendium of 29 projects sponsored by the U. S. Department of Education most of which contain instruments that can be used in the analysis of teacher education field experiences, student teaching, and entry year internships.

412. Newport, John F. *Constrasting Two Approaches to Developing Teacher Education Programs and Evaluating Student Teachers.* 1986. ERIC, ED 270 396.

Compares and contrasts two approaches to measuring the effectiveness of teacher education programs through the evaluation of student teachers.

413. Newport, John F. "Users Approve of a New Way to Evaluate Student Teachers." *Clearing House* 55 no. 9 (May 1982): 414-416.

Reports on the development of a form for evaluating student teachers that is designed to encourage them to develop their own teaching style.

414. O'Neal, Sharon F. *Supervision of Student Teachers: Feedback and Evaluation, Clinical Teacher Education.* 1983. ERIC, ED 240 106.

     Reports on the content of supervisory conferences and formal, final evaluations are compared to university protocols regarding the formative and summative evaluation of student teachers.

415. Pannell, Mary Sue. "A Model To Assess The Impact of Educational Field Experiences Upon Cooperating Schools." Ph.D. dissertation, Texas A & M University, 1985.

     Reviews the validation of a model for assessing the impact of programs of field experiences upon cooperating schools.

416. Partington, John. "Teachers in School as Teaching Practice Supervisors." *Journal of Education for Teaching* 8 no. 3 (October 1982): 262-274.

     Outlines the effects of school-based supervision and evaluation rather than a university-based system of student teaching supervision at schools where preservice teachers were practice teaching.

417. Pasch, Marvin, and others. *Collaboration for the Improvement of Teacher Education: A Preliminary Report.* 1988. ERIC, ED 290 732.

     Outlines a program titled "Collaboration for the Improvement of Teacher Education" which is designed to bring university and school personnel together to create, implement, and assess structured pre-student teaching field experiences to accompany a newly implemented core teacher education program.

418. Payne, Beverly Dean. "Interrelationships Among College Supervisor, Supervising Teacher, and Elementary Pupil Ratings of Student Teaching Performance." *Educational and Psychological Measurement* 44 no. 4 (Winter 1984): 1037-1043.

     Outlines the validity of elementary school pupil ratings of the teaching performance of student teachers using nine competencies from the Teacher Performance Assessment Instruments, with ratings by college supervisors and supervising teachers serving as criteria for contrast of validity coefficients of student ratings.

419. Pease, David W. "Quis Custodiet Custodes?" *Teacher Educator* 12 no. 1 (1976): 26-30.

    Outlines the use of a student teacher evaluation instrument designed to assess the characteristics most valued in the university supervisor, answering the question posed in the title: Who Will Guard the Guardians?

420. Perl, Michael, and Nancy A. Starke. *Pre-Professional Laboratory Experiences: A Handbook for Students.* 1984. ERIC, ED 262 034. (See also ED 262 035.)

    Describes a handbook for use in pre-professional laboratory experiences that contains extensive systems for evaluation of all aspects of the program for use in improving teacher education programs.

421. Perl, Michael, and Nancy A. Starke. *Pre-Professional Laboratory Experiences: A Handbook for Teachers.* 1984. ERIC, ED 262 035. (See also ED 262 034.)

    Describes a handbook designed for teachers involved in pre-professional laboratory experiences, which includes extensive evaluation materials useful for teacher education program improvement.

422. Peters, Jerry L., and Gary L. Moore. *A Comparison of Two Methods of Providing Laboratory Teaching Experience for Student Teachers in Agricultural Education.* 1980. ERIC, ED 210 468.

    Outlines the results and evaluation of a comparative study of microteaching and reflective teaching in preparing agricultural education student teachers.

423. Pfister, Jill, and L. H. Newcomb. *Evaluation of the Student Teaching Program in Agricultural Education at The Ohio State University.* 1984. ERIC, ED 239 097.

    Describes the student teaching program evaluation at The Ohio State University which consists of a comprehensive model collecting assessment data from such sources as supervisors, cooperating teachers, and student teachers.

424. Phelps, LeAdelle, and others. "The Effects of Halo and Leniency on Cooperating Teacher Reports Using Likert-Type Rating Scales." *Journal of Educational Research* 79 no. 3 (January/February 1986): 151-154.

Reports the use of a Likert-type scale cooperating report on student teachers which demonstrated a significant presence of leniency error and halo effect, leaving highly questionable the validity of the report as a whole.

425. Pisoni, Charles Joseph. "A Comparative Factor Analysis of the Impact of Two Student Teaching Programs upon the Schools of Michigan with Implications for the Evaluation of Teacher Education Programs." Ph.D. dissertation, Michigan State University, 1977.

Examines the impact the Central Michigan University student teaching program had on cooperating schools in 1969 and 1973.

426. Pope, Carol Ann. "The Relationship Between Student Teachers' and Cooperating Teachers' Educational Beliefs and Their Perceptions of the Student Teaching Experience." Ed.D. dissertation, University of Virginia, 1983.

Investigates whether student teachers and cooperating teachers who had similar educational beliefs would perceive the student teaching experience more positively than student teachers and cooperating teachers who had dissimilar educational beliefs.

427. Powell, Marjorie, and Joseph W. Beard. *Teacher Attitudes.* New York: Garland Publishing, 1986.

Includes annotated references to over 1,900 documents related to teacher attitudes which may be of use in evaluating laboratory experiences in a teacher education program.

428. Powell, Marjorie, and Joseph W. Beard. *Teacher Effectiveness.* New York: Garland Publishing, 1984.

   Includes over 3,000 annotated references to teacher effectiveness that may be useful in evaluating laboratory experience programs and determining the effects of a teacher education program.

429. Purcell, Thomas D., and Berniece B. Seiferth. *Student Teacher Educational Values: Changes Resulting from Student Teaching.* 1981. ERIC, ED 220 460.

   Reports the results of a study of the attitudes of student teachers before and after their field experiences.

430. Quinn, Peter J. *Do Field Experiences Make a Difference in the Training of Pre-Service Education Students? Let's Find Out!* 1986. ERIC, ED 278 634.

   Reviews teacher education-related events and research regarding the role of field experiences in the preparation of prospective teachers and presents a questionnaire designed to elicit attitudes of teacher educators toward the role of field experiences in teacher preparation programs.

431. Reh, Rita Anne. "An Assessment of Student Teachers' Knowledge and Performance Related To The Development and Management of An Integrated Unit." Ed.D. dissertation, University of Pittsburgh, 1976.

   Looks at the value and desirability of certain integrated courses of study in operation thereby testing both theory and practice.

432. Reiff, Judith C. "Evaluating Student Teacher Effectiveness." *College Student Journal* 14 no. 4 (Winter 1980): 369-372.

   Describes the Teacher Performance Assessment Instruments and shows the relationship to ratings of student teacher performance made by supervising teachers and pupils.

433. Robertson, Blaine P. *Student Teacher Evaluation: Development of a Summative Evaluation Instrument for Use at the Secondary Level.* 1986. ERIC, ED 271 420.

     Outlines the development and use of an instrument to be used in the summative evaluations of secondary student teachers.

434. Rohe, C. James. "Toward a Model for Improving the Professional Quality of the Student Teaching Practicum." Ed.D. dissertation, University of Illinois at Urbana-Champaign, 1984.

     Develops a model to help colleges or departments of education structure and focus the student teaching practicum.

435. Rubin, Sharon. *Performance Appraisal: A Guide to Better Supervisor Evaluation Processes.* 1982. ERIC, ED 260 634.

     Describes the importance of evaluating student interns as a part of a regular performance appraisal for all employees and the role of the internship coordinator or faculty sponsor in the total evaluation process.

436. Rutanawilai, Saowaporn. "The Outcomes of the Use of a Structured Observation Scale in Supervising Secondary Student Teachers." Ph.D. dissertation, Oregon State University, 1983.

     Examines the effects of structured observation of student teachers on their performance in the classroom.

437. Sanford, Julie P., and Edmund T. Emmer. *Understanding Classroom Management: An Observation Guide.* Englewood Cliffs, NJ: Prentice-Hall, 1988.

     Outlines observational inventories to collect data on the progress of teacher candidates throughout their field experience programs.

438. Saslaw, Rita, and others. *Field Experiences in Educational Foundations: An Evaluation of a New Component of Teacher Education.* 1983. ERIC, ED 231 770.

     Outlines a study of how a new experience component in education foundations' core course work can be evaluated and used for program improvement.

439. Schivley, Warren Wendell. "Relationship of Teacher Candidate Measures to Student Teaching Rating and Quality Point Average." D.Ed. dissertation, The Pennsylvania State University, 1976.

    Examines the relationship between student teaching success and thirteen predictor variables.

440. Schofer, Gilliam. "Goal-Setting as a Teaching and Evaluation Tool in Student Teaching." *College Student Journal* 15 no. 4 (Winter 1981): 295-298.

    Analyzes the stated goals of participants in student teaching and describes a system for use in evaluating goal achievement.

441. Scholl, Robert L. *Linking Pre-Service and In-Service Teacher Self-Assessment: A Model for Instructional Improvement.* 1984. ERIC, ED 241 460.

    Offers a model for evaluation of both pre-service and in-service teachers in an integrated manner that begins with student teaching and progress through the time of employment as a teacher and there after.

442. Seiferthy, Berniece B., and Marie Samuel. *A Survey of Attitudinal Changes of Student Teachers in Fine Arts.* 1979. ERIC, ED 177 084.

    Reports the results of a survey to determine the attitudes of fine arts student teachers toward 20 educational concepts before and after their student teaching experience are reported.

443. Shahzade, Joyce Burton. "The Match of Style and Conceptual Level of University Supervisors with Student Teachers in Relationship to Supervisor Effectiveness." Ed.D. dissertation, University of the Pacific, 1983.

    Investigates the relationships that exist between the supervisorial style and conceptual level of university supervisors and the student teachers supervised at two university sites in California.

444. Shaw, Stan F. "A Preservice Perspective on Quality Training in Special Education." *B. C. Journal of Special Education* 10 no. 3 (1986): 243-249.

    Discusses program components, training philosophy, and student and program evaluation criteria of a special education undergraduate teacher training program, with emphasis on field experience programs.

445. Shulman, Judith H., and Joel A. Colbert, eds. *The Mentor Teacher Casebook.* 1987. ERIC, ED 291 153.

    Outlines a series of case studies of beginning teachers as perceived by mentor teachers, including evaluation and suggested sources of additional information.

446. Shulman, Judith H., and Joel A. Colbert, eds. *The Intern Teacher Casebook.* 1988. ERIC, ED 296 998.

    Presents candid descriptions of teachers who enter the profession with no previous teacher preparation and how to deal with preparing the individuals to work in the classroom.

447. Silvernail, David L. *Assessing the Effectiveness of Preservice Field Experiences in Reducing Teacher Anxiety and Concern Levels.* 1980. ERIC, ED 191 828.

    Reports the results of a study to determine if preservice internship programs were more effective than a student teacher program in reducing beginning teacher anxiety and concern levels.

448. Simmons, Joanne M. *"Wha'd She Think?"--A Comparison of the Role Perspectives, Evaluative Judgment Criteria Cognitive Maps, & Written Records of Three University Student Teacher Supervisors.* 1988. ERIC, ED 293 808.

    Describes case study methodology using structured interviewing and cognitive mapping techniques to reveal the contrasting role perspectives and evaluative judgment criteria of three university student teacher supervisors with different professional backgrounds.

449. Simmons, Joanne M., and others. *Collaboration for the Improvement of Teacher Education (CITE) Project. Data Collection Plan & Instruments 1987-88/Year 3*. 1987. ERIC, ED 289 824.

    Examines the Collaboration for the Improvement of Teacher Education Project which includes extensive field experiences and a system for evaluation of these experiences.

450. Sluce, P. M. "Determining Objectives for Placements." *Assessment and Evaluation in Higher Education* 12 no. 2 (Summer 1987): 123-135.

    Investigates the usefulness of identifying priorities and coordinating specific employer, teacher, and student objectives in placing home economics undergraduate students in supervised work experience programs.

451. Smith, C. Leland, and J. Truman Stevens. "A Criterion-Referenced Evaluation of Student Teachers in Science." *School Science and Mathematics* 84 no. 2 (February 1984): 125-135.

    Describes the development of a procedure for evaluating student teaching in science, presenting criteria for criterion referenced evaluation, organizing principles for the evaluation format, and application format.

452. Smith, Gwen Cornelius. "A Study of Change in Selected Student Teachers' Attitudes During the Student Teaching Experience." Ed.D. dissertation, The University of Alabama, 1983.

    Investigates attitudinal changes in selected student teachers during a period of student teaching at the University of Alabama.

453. Smith, Lynn C. and Donna E. Alvermann. *Field-Experience Reading Interns Profile the Effective/Ineffective University Supervisor*. 1983. ERIC, ED 237 964.

    Examines students' perceptions of what distinguishes effective from ineffective university supervision in field experience programs in reading.

454. Smith, Mary Ann Maines. "Leadership and Learning Styles of Cooperating Teachers and Student Teachers as Related To Communication During Student Teaching." Ph.D. dissertation, University of Minnesota, 1981.

Investigates the ways student teachers and cooperating teachers matched or mismatched on leadership style and learning style/conceptual level communicated.

455. Solliday, Michael A. "The University Supervisor: A Double Image." *Teacher Educator* 18 no. 3 (Winter 1982/83): 11-15.

Reports the findings from a survey which provides data about student teacher supervisors concerning the duties they perform, their supervising load, academic rank, and the evaluation of student teacher supervisors.

456. Spaulding, Robert L. "Generalizability of Teacher Behavior: Stability of Observational Data Within and Across Facets of Classroom Environments." *Journal of Educational Research* 76 no. 1 (September/October 1982): 5-13.

Examines the reliability and stability of teacher behavior scores as measured by the Spaulding Teacher Activity Recording Schedule utilizing a student teacher at work in a campus laboratory setting and in a primary ungraded classroom.

457. Stanard, Marilynn. "West Virginia's Professional Education Performance Assessments: Quilt or Patches?" *Action in Teacher Education* 7 no. 1/2 (Spring/Summer 1985): 31-40.

Reviews the professional performance assessment of student teachers in field based programs in West Virginia and suggests ways to incorporate the evaluations into teacher education program improvement.

458. Steinberger, Marcia Lee. "The Impact of Student Teaching Upon Teaching Perspectives." Ed.D. dissertation, University of Pittsburgh, 1984.

Describes the results of a study to determine perspectives on pupil control and teaching concerns change during student teaching and if so, in what direction.

459. Stevens, J. Truman, and C. Lealand Smith. "Supervising Teacher Accountability: Evaluation by the Student Teacher." *Peabody Journal of Education* 56 no. 1 (October 1978): 64-74.

Describes procedures for developing a validated instrument to solicit evaluative feedback from student teachers regarding the performance of supervising teachers.

460. Stewart, Mendel Harold. "A Study of the Performance and Skills of Clemson University Student Teachers During Practice Teaching." Ed.D. dissertation, University of South Carolina, 1984.

Reports the performance and skills of student teachers from Clemson University and determines if there were differences at various intervals of practice teaching.

461. Stieglitz, Ezra L., and others. *Right to Read Preservice Teacher Preparation Project. A Competency-Based Teacher Education Model.* 1976. ERIC, ED 129 756.

Outlines a variety of ways of evaluating all aspects of a student teaching program and utilizing the information for teacher education program improvement.

462. Stupiansky, Nicholas G. "Interrelationships of Performance in Early Field Experiences and Student Teaching, Grade Point Average, and Success in Obtaining Employment as a Teacher." Ph.D. dissertation, Indiana University, 1984.

Describes the relationships between predictor variables and performance, best and poorest performing student teacher, and pursuers and nonpursuers of teaching positions.

463. Tabachnick, B. Robert, and Kenneth M. Zeichner. "The Impact of the Student Teaching Experience on the Development of Teacher Perspectives." *Journal of Teacher Education* 35 no. 6 (November/December 1984): 28-36.

Reports the influence of student teaching in the teacher socialization process and reports that the process gives direction to socialization but does not determine outcome.

464. Tanner, David E. "The Theory/Practice "Double Bind" in Student Teaching." *Teacher Education and Practice* 4 no. 1 (Spring/Summer 1987): 45-49.

     Reports a study which was conducted to establish the degree of uniformity that exists between the university supervisor, the cooperating teacher, and the student teacher in evaluating the student teacher according to common criteria.

465. Thies-Sprinthall, L. "Promoting the Developmental Growth of Supervising Teachers: Theory, Research Programs, and Implications." *Journal of Teacher Education* 35 no. 3 (May/June 1984): 53-60.

     Examines the evaluation and results of a pilot study of supervising teachers enrolled in a course to increase flexibility in supervision through role taking experiences.

466. Thies-Sprinthall, Lois. "Supervision: An Educative or Mis-Educative Process?" *Journal of Teacher Education* 31 no. 4 (July/August 1980): 17-20.

     Reports the use of direct classroom observation techniques and other instruments with student teachers in order to provide a comprehensive system for evaluation.

467. Tinning, Richard I. *Supervision of Student Teaching: A Behavioral Critique.* 1983. ERIC, ED 227 082.

     Reviews the literature and evaluates the efficacy of university faculty as supervisors of student teachers and concludes that university supervisors have a low impact on student teachers, and that their role is secondary to that of cooperating teachers.

468. Tinning, Richard Irving. "A Task Theory of Student Teaching: Development and Provisional Testing." Ph.D. dissertation, The Ohio State University, 1983.

     Reviews the development of a task theory of student teaching based on the concepts of task originally articulated by Walter Doyle.

469. Twa, Jim, and others. *Testing Models Developed to Predict Performance in Student Teaching.* 1980. ERIC, ED 193 198.

    Reports the results of a study to validate on a second sample of student teachers, prediction equations developed to predict performance in student teaching.

470. Van Cleaf, D., and L. Schade. "Student Teacher Learning Styles: Another Dimension of Reform." *Teacher Education and Practice* 4 no. 1 (1987): 22-25.

    Examines the relationship between learning styles of student teachers, their selected teaching areas, and their classroom performance.

471. Vukovich, Diane. *The Effects of Four Specific Supervision Procedures on the Development of Self-Evaluation Skills in Pre-Service Teachers.* 1976. ERIC, ED 146 224.

    Examines the effect of the direct versus indirect method of supervision and the influence of one versus three prior self-evaluation experiences on the self-evaluation of preservice teachers and outlines some implications for improving preservice teacher education programs.

472. Webb, Mary Smith. "Conflict in the Supervisory Triad of College Supervisor, Cooperating Teacher and Student Teacher." Ph.D. dissertation, University of Oregon, 1979.

    Examines conflict as it occurs between and among student teacher, cooperating teacher, and college supervisor.

473. Wheeler, A. E., and H. R. Knoop. "Self, Teacher and Faculty Assessments of Student Teaching Performance." *Journal of Educational Research* 75 no. 3 (January/February 1982): 178-181.

    Reports the results of a comparison of the assessments of student teaching performance by the student teachers, cooperating teachers, and supervising teachers.

474. Wheeler, Mary Anne, and others. "STEM: An Interactive Approach for Training and Evaluating Teacher Trainees in Special Education." *Teacher Education and Special Education* 8 no. 1 (Winter 1985): 33-40.

Outlines the development, field testing, and revision of a comptency-based program guide and interactive evaluation system to prepare preservice teachers in special education.

475. Whiddon, Sue, and others. *A Competency Chart for Evaluating Student Teachers in Physical Education.* 1978. ERIC, ED 161 836.

Describes a systems approach that includes evaluation devices for evaluating student teachers of physical education.

476. Whoolever, Roberta. *Observing Student Teachers for a Hierachy of Generic Teaching Skills.* 1983. ERIC, ED 238 839.

Describes an approach to supervision and evaluation of student teachers that includes identification of generic teaching competencies and a systematic appraisal with reference to established desirable teaching behaviors.

477. Wood, Martha Ellen. "A Comparative Study of Student Teaching Program Practices in Institutions of Higher Education in the Upper Midwest." Ed.D. dissertation, University of South Dakota, 1986.

Surveyed institutions in a seven state area to determine which ones met the Johnson and Yates (1981) twenty-four criteria of the best student teaching program.

478. Yore, Larry D., and others. *Reflective-Responsive Evaluation Techniques for Undergraduate Pre-Service Science Teacher Education Programs.* 1979. ERIC, ED 243 852.

Outlines the development and implementation of a comprehensive evaluation plan for all types of field experience programs.

479. Zeichner, Kenneth M. "Alternative Paradigms of Teacher Education." *Journal of Teacher Education* 31 no. 6 (May/June 1983): 3-9.

    Provides an outline of several alternative paradigms for conducting teacher education programs and the operation of laboratory experiences programs.

480. Zeichner, Kenneth M. "The Ecology of Field Experience: Toward an Understanding of the Role of Field Experiences in Teacher Development." In *Advances in Teacher Education, Volume 3*, edited by Martin Haberman and Julie M. Backus, 94-117. Norwood, NJ: Ablex Publishing Company, 1987.

    Outlines the use of field experiences in teacher education programs and provides suggestions for the evaluation and improvement of programs.

481. Zeichner, Kenneth M. "Myths and Realities: Field-Based Experiences in Preservice Teacher Education." *Journal of Teacher Education* 31 no. 6 (November/December 1980): 45-49.

    Discusses the myths and realities of field-based experiences in the preservice teacher education program, including ways to evaluate the programs.

482. Zimpher, Nancy L. "Current Trends in Research on University Supervision of Student Teaching." In *Advances in Teacher Education, Volume 3*, eds. Martin Haberman and Julie M. Backus, 118-150. Norwood, NJ: Ablex Publishing Company, 1987.

    Outlines and summarizes a variety of research studies related to the university supervision of student teachers.

483. Zimpher, Nancy L., and Kenneth R. Howey. "Adapting Supervisory Practices to Different Orientations of Teaching Competence." *Journal of Curriculum and Supervision* 2 no. 2 (1986): 101-127.

    Outlines the use of different types of supervisory practices with different types of orientations of teaching competence.

484. Zimpher, Nancy L., and others. "A Closer Look at University Teacher Supervision." *Journal of Teacher Education* 31 no. 4 (July/August 1980): 11-51.

Examines the role of the university based supervisor in the student-teacher process including the role of the individual in providing input for program development and evaluation.

485. Zimper, Nancy L., and Susan R. Rieger. *Using Research to Improve Teacher Education: Implementation of an Induction Program for Inquiring Professionals.* Washington, D. C.: Office of Educational Research and Improvement, U. S. Department of Education, 1988.

Describes the development and field testing of a package of evaluation instruments for use in evaluating beginning teachers; however, the package has equal value in the assessment of student teaching programs.

Outcomes Assessment

486. Adelman, Clifford, ed. *Assessment in American Higher Education. Issues and Contexts.* 1986. ERIC, ED 273 197.

Emerging and traditional forms of outcomes assessment in U.S. higher education are considered in the five conference papers included in the document.

487. Adelman, Clifford. *The Standardized Test Scores of College Graduates, 1964-1982.* 1984. ERIC, ED 248 827.

Scores from 23 standardized tests used in applications to graduate and professional schools are analyzed and conclusions presented.

488. Adelman, Clifford, and Elaine Reuben. *Starting with Students: Notable Programs, Promising Approaches, and Other Improvement Efforts in American Postsecondary Education.* 1984. ERIC, ED 255 169.

Describes 66 notable programs and promising practices related to specific problems, practices, and goals in American postsecondary education and also discusses assessment of outcomes.

489. Andrews, Jerry W., and others. "Preservice Performance and the National Teacher Exams." *Phi Delta Kappan* 61 no. 5 (January 1980): 358-359.

Indicates that the sparsity of significant positive relationships between the National Teacher Examinations (NTE) scores and teaching performance ratings, when coupled with the presence of a few significant negative relationships, tends to undermine confidence in the relationship of NTE scores to teaching performance ratings.

490. Ansah, S. L. *Quality Teachers: Is Testing the Answer?* 1985. ERIC, ED 265 211.

Offers reasons to de-emphasize testing as a means of assessing teacher outcomes quality.

491. Armstrong, Elizabeth Phyllis. "Educational Outcome Assessment and Its Use in the Accreditation Process: Current Developments and Future Feasibility." Ph.D. dissertation, Claremont Graduate School, 1983.

Discusses actions taken by accrediting agencies and postsecondary institutions to change their evaluations to ones which consider educational accomplishment and performance outcomes.

492. Astin, Alexander W. "Measuring the Outcomes of Higher Education." *New Directions for Institutional Research* 1 (1974): 23-46.

Examines the use of outcomes assessment in higher education as a means of assessing institutional impact and encourages the development and use of relative measures of student outcomes.

493. Astin, Alexander W., and Frank Ayala. "Institutional Strategies: A Consortial Approach to Assessment." *Educational Record* 68 no. 3 (Summer 1987): 47-51.

    Reports the results of implementing a value-added approach to assessing student progress and development and indicates that the most significant finding of the project was the importance of having a good institutional database on students.

494. Ayers, Jerry B. "Another Look at the Concurrent and Predictive Validity of the National Teacher Examinations." *Journal of Educational Research* 81 no. 3 (January/February 1988): 133-137.

    Examines the concurrent validity of the NTE in predicting success as an undergraduate and the predictive validity of the NTE in relationship to classroom performance.

495. Ayers, Jerry B., and Glenda S. Qualls. "Concurrent and Predictive Validity of the National Teacher Examinations." *Journal of Educational Research* 73 no. 2 (November/December 1979): 86-92.

    Reports the results of a study of the concurrent and predictive validity of the National Teacher Examinations in relationship to success in the classroom.

496. Ayres, Q. Whitfield. "Student Achievement at Predominantly White and Predominantly Black Universities." *American Educational Research Journal* 20 no. 2 (Summer 1983): 291-304.

    Compares the results of administering the National Teacher Examinations at predominantly white and predominantly black institutions and concludes that students at the former achieved higher scores on the test.

497. Banks, Ivan Winslow. "The Beginning Teacher Evaluation Instrument and Its Relationship To The National Teacher Examinations." Ed.D. dissertation, University of Kentucky, 1983.

    Investigates the Beginning Teacher Evaluation instrument, its reliability and relationship to the NTE, and the usefulness of it as an observational tool.

498. Benton, Sidney E., and Bob W. Jerrolds. *The Relationship of Graduate Education Students' Achievement in Educational Research to Their Reading Attitudes, Attitudes Toward Educational Research, GPAs, and National Teacher Examinations.* 1983. ERIC, ED 238 929.

   Reviews the use of the National Teacher Examinations scores and other variables in predicting the success of students in a course in educational research.

499. Birlem, Lynne M. "Testing the Competency of Teachers: A Brief Bibliography." *Education Libraries* 5 no. 1 (Fall 1979): 13.

   Includes a brief bibliography of references to articles concerning competency testing of teachers and the use of the National Teacher Examinations.

500. Capie, W., and others. *Teacher Performance Assessment Instruments.* 1979. ERIC, ED 182 518.

   Describes an approach to and instruments for the evaluation of students as they exit from teacher education programs and begin teaching.

501. Clawson, Kenneth. *Teacher Education Students: A Look at Basic Skills Admission Tests and National Teacher Examination Scores.* 1986. ERIC, ED 279 717.

   Explores the relationships of outcomes assessment measures (National Teacher Examinations) to scores from entrance level admission and counseling tests.

502. Claxton, Charles, and others. "Outcomes Assessment." *AGB Reports* 29 no. 5 (September/October 1987): 32-35.

   Identifies seven characteristics of an effective outcomes assessment program and indicates that outcomes assessment is a curricular rather than a measurement issue.

503. Cross, L. H. "Validation of the NTE Tests for Certification Decisions." *Educational Measurement* 4 (1985): 7-10.

   Discusses the use of the National Teacher Examinations in making decisions about licensure as a teacher.

504. Ejlali, Christine M. Sosnowski. "The Relationship Among Selected Variables of University and Teacher Education Admission Criteria and Scores on the Common Examination of the National Teacher Examination." Ed.D. dissertation, East Tennessee State University, 1982.

   Examines the relationships among selected variables which best predict scores on the National Teacher Examinations-Weighted Common Examination Total Score.

505. Ewell, Peter T. "Establishing a Campus-Based Assessment Program." *New Directions for Higher Education* 15 no. 3 (Fall 1987): 9-24.

   Outlines steps in developing and establishing an outcomes assessment program, emphasizing the purposes of assessment.

506. Facione, P. A. "A Vision for Teacher Education." *Teacher Education Quarterly* 12 no. 4 (1985): 75-83.

   Lists the ideal attributes of teacher candidates before and after completing a teacher preparation program and recommends ways to improve training and professionalize teaching.

507. Grambling State University. *Teacher Education Improvement Project 1985-1986.* 1986. ERIC, ED 277 674.

   Documents the change process that was used by one institution to improve its teacher education programs with particular emphasis on increasing student scores on outcomes assessment tests.

508. Griffith, Susan R. *Using the Results of a State-Mandated Student Outcomes Assessment Test to Reevaluate Curriculum and Policies: A Case Study.* 1988. ERIC, ED 298 865.

Examines the effects of a state-mandated student outcomes assessment program on the teacher education program at one institution.

509. Halpern, Diane F. "Recommendations and Caveats." *New Directions for Higher Education* 15 no. 3 (Fall 1987): 109-111.

Lists eight topics in planning and implementing outcomes-focused assessment, including the findings that multiple measures are more desirable than a single standard examination; faculty involvement is essential; and performance-based funding should be derived from additional resources.

510. Harris, John. *Assessing Outcomes in Higher Education: Practical Suggestions for Getting Started.* 1985. ERIC, ED 260 677.

Provides a list of suggestions for developing and implementing an outcomes assessment program in higher education.

511. Harris, John. "Assessing Outcomes in Higher Education." In *Assessment in American Higher Education*, ed. C. Adelman, 13-31. Washington: U. S. Government Printing Office, 1986.

Summarizes a number of issues related to assessing the outcomes of higher education.

512. Hoffman, Janet, and David Dunnington. *Use of Exit Surveys at the University of Washington.* 1987. ERIC, ED 289 432.

Describes the use of exit surveys at the University of Washington for improving programs for the preparation of students in a variety of areas.

513. Katz, Lilian G., and James D. Raths. *Dispositional Goals for Teacher Education: Problems of Identification and Assessment.* 1986. ERIC, ED 272 470.

    Defines and reviews the use and assessment of dispositional goals as a tool for determining the outcomes of a teacher education program.

514. Lovelace, Terry, and Charles E. Martin. *The Revised National Teacher Examinations as a Predictor of Teachers' Performance in Public School Classrooms.* 1984. ERIC, ED 251 416.

    Reports that predictions of teaching performance as measured by the Teacher Performance Assessment Instrument utilizing the National Teacher Examinations scores, American College Test scores, grade point averages, personal characteristics, and certification level are inconclusive and warrant further investigation.

515. Lynch, Estella Smith. "A Comparison of Two Early Childhood Teacher Education Programs to Determine the Relationship Between Program Characteristics and Student Exit Characteristics." Ed.D. dissertation, Memphis State University, 1977.

    Identifies the learning activities in which teacher education students participate and determine the knowledge and skills that result from these activities.

516. McCollester, Kenneth Elwin. "Prospective Teachers: Patterns of Exit and Entry." Ph.D. dissertation, The University of Arizona, 1980.

    Assesses the characteristics commonly associated with persistence in order to determine if these same characteristics predict success in teacher training programs.

517. McGrail, Janet, and others. *Looking at Schools. Instruments and Processes for School Analysis.* 1987. ERIC, ED 280 885.

    Presents a summary and analysis of a variety of instruments for use in measuring performance outcomes of teacher education program graduates.

518. McLaurin, Sidney Edward. "The Relationship Between Achievement on the National Teachers Examinations and Teaching Attitude for a Selected Group of Student Teachers at a Southern University." Ph.D. dissertation, University of Southern Mississippi, 1982.

    Reports the relationship between the criterion variable achievement on the NTE and the variables of sex and teaching attitude measured by the MTAI.

519. Medley, Donald M., and others. *Measurement-Based Evaluation of Teacher Performance*. New York: Longman Inc., 1984.

    Describes an empirically based approach to the evaluation of student teachers and other educational personnel in the classroom.

520. Olstad, Roger G. *The Relationship of NTE Exams to Teacher Education Admission, Performance, and Employment*. 1988. ERIC, ED 291 698.

    Reports the results of a study of the National Teacher Examinations scores as predictors of success in student teaching.

521. Olstad, Roger G., and others. *Predictive Validity of GPA, CAT and NTE Science Speciality Tests on Scores of a Performance Based Student Teaching Evaluation Instrument*. 1987. ERIC, ED 282 761.

    Reports the results of the use of the National Teacher Examinations speciality area test in science as a predictor of success in the classroom.

522. Panackal, Abraham A. *Basic Studies Program and General Education Program in a College of Education: Achievement of Students in the College and National Teacher Examinations*. 1975. ERIC, ED 123 206.

    Discusses the relative merits of various types of programs for the preparation of teachers and notes that students in a more rigid program of study achieve higher scores on the National Teacher Examinations.

523. Panackal, Abraham A. "Rigid and Flexible Course Requirements and Achievements in a College of Education." *College Student Journal* 14 no. 2 (Summer 1980): 135-141.

Indicates that when course selection requirements were made flexible in a college of education, the graduates who follow the flexible program achieved lower scores on the National Teacher Examinations Mathematics sub-test and did not achieve higher cumulative grade point averages in the college when compared to those who followed a more rigid program of study.

524. Peck, Hugh I. *The Effects of the Level of Content Preparation on the Performance of Mathematics Teachers on Their NTE Specialty Area Examination.* 1987. ERIC, ED 291 786.

Reports that the level of achievement on the Mathematics Specialty Area Test of the National Teacher Examinations was directly related to the number of hours of mathematics taken as a part of the teacher preparation program and was not related to achievement on the General Knowledge portion of the test.

525. Poggio, J. P., and others. "Strategies for Validating Teacher Certification Tests." *Educational Measurement* 5 (1986): 18-25.

Outlines various strategies for validating teacher certification tests which may have application in the outcomes assessment of teacher education programs.

526. Popham, W. James. "The Shortcomings of Champagne Teacher Evaluations." *Journal of Personnel Evaluation in Education* 1 no. 1 (1987): 25-28.

Advocates the use of professional judgment as one tool in determining the effectiveness of teachers and teacher education programs.

527. Pratt, Linda K., and others. *The Relationship of the Myers-Briggs Type Indicator to Scores on the National Teacher Examinations.* 1981. ERIC, ED 205 128.

Examines the use of the Myers-Briggs Type Indicator test as a predictor of achievement on the National Teacher Examinations and concludes that there are some relationships that should be examined further.

528. Pratt, Linda K., and others. *Predicting Student Performance on the Professional Knowledge Portion of the NTE Core Battery.* 1987. ERIC, ED 290 398.

   Describes the development of a set of regression equations to predict the success of students on the Professional Knowledge portion of the National Teacher Examinations core battery.

529. Pultorak, Edward George. "Effectiveness of GPA, Student Teacher Evaluation, and Subject Matter Major as Predictors of Achievement for Secondary Teacher Education Candidates on Core Battery Tests of the National Teachers Examination." Ph.D. dissertation, Indiana State University, 1988.

   Investigates the effectiveness of grade point average, student teacher evaluation, and subject matter major as predictors of achievement on the National Teacher Examinations.

530. Rosner, Frieda C., and Kenneth R. Howey. "Construct Validity in Assessing Teacher Knowledge: New NTE Interpretations." *Journal of Teacher Education* 33 no. 6 (November/December 1982): 7-12.

   Reports changes in the professional knowledge, general knowledge, and communication skills components of the National Teacher Examinations and explains validation procedures.

531. Rudner, Lawrence M., and Thomas E. Eissenberg. *Standard Setting Practices for Teacher Tests.* 1988. ERIC, ED 293 865.

   Examines the use of the National Teacher Examinations as a licensure requirement and as a requirement for graduation from teacher education programs.

532. Schnur, James O. and others. "Outcomes Based Teacher Education." *Action in Teacher Education* 9 no. 3 (Fall 1987): 25-32.

   Describes an automated student performance monitoring system that includes performance assessments by observation.

533. Scriven, Michael. "Duty-Based Teacher Education." *Journal of Personnel Evaluation in Education* 1 no. 4 (1988): 319-334.

   Explores various ways of evaluating the outcomes of a teacher education program.

534. Sheehan, Daniel S., and Mary Marcus. "Teacher Performance on the National Teacher Examinations and Student Mathematics and Vocabulary Achievement." *Journal of Educational Research* 71 no. 3 (1978): 134-136.

   Analyzes the National Teacher Examinations and shows that the weighted common examination scores are significant predictors of effective teaching (student achievement), if the variance shared with teacher race is included.

535. Shelton, Aubrey W., and others. *A Longitudinal Study of Pre- and Post-Reform ACT Data on Elementary Education Majors.* 1987. ERIC, ED 291 718.

   Examines the impact of the Mississippi Legislative Reform Act on elementary education majors and reports the relationships between scores from the National Teacher Examinations, the American College Test and the State of Mississippi's College Outcomes Measures Program.

536. Stoller, Jane E., and Victor L. Willson. *Predicting Teacher NTE Scores in Mathematics.* 1977. ERIC, ED 161 682.

   Summarizes a research study in which it was found that scores on the Mathematics Test of the National Teacher Examinations coupled with hours of credit in college mathematics and grade level of teaching accounted for 61 percent of the variance in observed NTE scores.

537. Tarver, Linda K. *A Study of Selected Variables Involved in the Assessment of Teacher Proficiency.* 1982. ERIC, ED 218 333.

   Describes the results of a study to determine the performance of Louisiana's prospective teachers on the Common Examinations of the National Teacher Examinations in relation to national averages, and to determine strengths and weaknesses in the test performance of Louisiana's prospective teachers.

538. Tarver, Linda K., and Dan B. Carr. *Prospective Teachers'
Performance on the National Teacher Examinations and the
American College Test.* 1981. ERIC, ED 228 330.

Outlines the relationship between scores from the American
College Test and the National Teacher Examinations for
prospective teachers in the State of Louisiana.

539. Tollett, John Roland. "Relationship of Selected Variables to
Measures of Success in a Teacher Education Program." Ed.D.
dissertation, Northeast Louisiana University, 1980.

Looks at the relationship between personal high school,
scholastic and interaction variables, grade point average, and the
National Teacher Examinations.

540. Wendling, Laura M., and others. *The Effectiveness of a Narrow
Social Science Major in Preparing Students to Teach in the Broad
Field of Social Studies.* 1986. ERIC, ED 278 606.

Examines scores on the National Teacher Examinations from
students who have had a broad preparation in the social sciences in
comparison with students who have majored largely in one area and
concludes that there are no major differences in scores on the NTE.

541. Wiebe, Gordan. "The Character of Certification Tests and the
Relationship of These Tests to Factors Identified by Research
Literature of Education as Important for Teacher Success." Ph.D.
dissertation, Miami University, 1981.

Looks at the relationship of certification examinations to
factors identified by research literature in education relative to
teacher success.

542. Wiley, Patricia Davis, and Judith A. Boser. *A Comparison of
Reading Scores with Other Academic Measures among Students in
Two Post-Baccalaureate Teacher Preparation Programs.* 1987.
ERIC, ED 292 817.

Summarizes a comparative study of two fifth year teacher
education programs by examining participant scores from the Pre-
Professional Skills Tests and the National Teacher Examinations.

543. Willson, Victor L., and Jane E. Stoller. "Predicting Teacher NTE
     Scores in Mathematics and Science." *Educational and
     Psychological Measurement* 41 no. 2 (Summer 1981): 479-485.

     Determines estimates of the criterion-related validity for the
     National Teacher Examinations in mathematics and science and
     reports that the result indicate the science tests are not as useful as
     the mathematics tests as indicators of subject knowledge.

544. Wilson, Ann E. Jarvella. "Knowledge for Teachers: The National
     Teacher Examinations Program, 1940 to 1970." Ph.D.
     dissertation, The University of Wisconsin-Madison, 1984.

     Studies the historical development of the National Teacher
     Examinations from 1940 to 1970.

545. Wilson, Ann Jarvella. *Historical Issues of Validity and
     Validation: The National Teacher Examinations.* 1986. ERIC,
     ED 270 503.

     Investigates the 50-year history of the National Teacher
     Examinations and finds a continuity of test content and
     justification over the program's existence; a primacy of reliance
     upon logical or content validity; and a paradoxical relationship of
     the tests to teacher education curricula.

IV. MANAGEMENT AND GOVERNANCE

546. American Association of Colleges for Teacher Education. *Guidelines for the Preparation of Elementary Teachers.* 1988. ERIC, ED 297 000.

   Describes preservice preparation of elementary teachers and includes an examination of four critical areas in the program related to the world of practice, students, faculty, and governance.

547. Appingnani, Georgianna, and others, ed. *Policy for the Education of Educators: Issues and Implications.* 1981. ERIC, ED 196 923.

   Discusses the redesign and redirection of programs for the preparation of teachers.

548. Berneman, Louis Paul. "The Governance of Teacher Education: A Struggle for Responsibility and Control." Ed.D. dissertation, Columbia University Teachers College, 1977.

   Analyzes the perceptions of individuals regarding the governance of teacher education.

549. Cameron, Kim. "Critical Questions in Assessing Organizational Effectiveness." *Organizational Dynamics* 9 (Autumn 1980): 66-80.

   Lists critical questions that should be used in assessing the effectiveness of an organization such as a teacher education program.

550. Cushman, M. L. *Some Perspectives on the Governance of Teacher Education.* 1977. ERIC, ED 156 622.

     Explores the major role of colleges of education in the governance of teacher education programs.

551. Cushman, M. L. "Some Perspectives on the Governance of Teacher Education." *Journal of Teaching and Learning* 3, no. 3 (1978): 3-15.

     Presents a discussion and analysis of the factors that influence the governance structure for teacher education programs.

552. Duncan, Patricia H. *The Governance of Reading Education: A Position Paper.* 1983. ERIC, ED 237 965.

     Analyzes the governance structure of effective programs for the preparation of reading teachers.

553. Dunwell, Robert R. *The Work Group Survey: Assessing Organizational Climate in Higher Education.* 1981. ERIC, ED 201 223.

     Describes an evaluation study of the organizational climate and governance structure of a teacher education program.

554. Harris, Clifton S. *A University-Wide Approach to Teacher Education: School of Education Autonomy Abjured.* 1983. ERIC, ED 228 177.

     Examines a university-wide approach to the governance of teacher education programs and ways of evaluating the structure.

555. Hatfield, Robert. *A Conceptual Perspective of Teacher Education Programs.* 1988. ERIC, ED 294 833.

     Provides a model for a conceptual structure for a teacher education program including a suggested system for analyzing the governance structure.

556. Jones, Donald W., ed. *Governance & Leadership in Teacher Education.* 1983. ERIC, ED 228 192.

   Analyzes various systems of governance employed in teacher education programs.

557. Jones, Donald W., ed. *Revitalizing Teacher Education in the Mid-Eighties.* 1983. ERIC, ED 236 152.

   Examines various issues related to teacher education programs including an analysis of unit governance.

558. Khullar, Gurdeep S., and George A. Antonelli. *Comparative Analysis of the Basics of Teacher Education and Training.* 1983. ERIC, ED 242 672.

   Presents the results of a survey that compares and contrasts the attitudes and opinions of educators toward governance, content, student teaching, certification, and candidate selection in teacher education programs.

559. Krakower, Jack Y. *Assessing Organizational Effectiveness: Considerations and Procedures.* Boulder, CO: National Center for Higher Education Management Systems, 1985.

   Offers an assessment system for the organizational effectiveness of higher education programs.

560. MacNaughton, Robert H., and others. "When Less Seems Like More: Managing the Expanded Field Experience of the 80's." *Journal of Teacher Education* 1982, no. 5 (September/October 1982): 10-13.

   Analyzes the governance structure that must be present in the laboratory and field experience components of a teacher education program.

561. Millett, John D. *Management, Governance and Leadership: A Guide for College and University Administrators.* New York: AMACOM, 1980.

    Summarizes some perspectives on the management, governance, evaluation, and leadership of higher education, including teacher education programs.

562. Orlosky, Donald E., ed. *Society, Schools, and Teacher Preparation.* 1988. ERIC, ED 296 996.

    Recommends procedures for the preparation of teachers and an analysis of the governance structure of teacher education programs.

563. Roth, Robert A. *The Redesign of Teacher Education in the United States: External Strategies: Competency Testing and State Program Approval.* 1983. ERIC, ED 233 001.

    Analyzes the redesign of teacher education programs and explores the need for the development of an adequate system of governance.

564. Saunders, Nancy, and Bill Franklin. *Departments and Department Chairs: Organizational and Administrative Influences on Undergraduate Teaching.* 1977, ERIC, ED 140 701.

    Examines, through an annotated bibliography, the ways in which the administrative structure of an institution influences undergraduate teaching.

565. Schneider, Barbara L., and others. "The Deans' Perspective on the Status of Doctoral Programs in Schools of Education." *Phi Delta Kappan* 65, no. 9 (May 1984): 617-620.

    Summarizes the results of a survey of Deans of doctoral programs in education which emphasized program governance, finances, evaluation, and relationships with other units of the institution.

566. Spencer, Richard L. "Planning and the Future of Institutional Research." *New Directions for Institutional Research* 6, no. 3 (1979): 69-72.

    Discusses the role of institutional research and its influences on the organization and governance of higher education.

567. Wheeler, Alan H. *Response to the Need for Quality: The School of Education at Radford.* 1983. ERIC, ED 237 510.

    Describes changes that have been made in one teacher education program in order to meet NCATE standards related to governance and other issues.

568. Wideen, Marvin F., and Patricia Holborn. *Program and Organizational Change in Faculties of Education: Some Lessons for Survival.* 1984. ERIC, ED 246 044.

    Presents the results of a study of governance in higher education that could effect teacher education programs.

569. Yarger, Sam J., and Bruce R. Joyce. "Going Beyond the Data: Reconstructing Teacher Education." *Journal of Teacher Education* 28, no. 6 (1977): 21-25.

    Interprets responses to a national survey on teacher education which indicate that governance, research and development, substantive improvement of education, and staff development need to be conceived as a totality.

V. RESOURCES

Faculty

570. Abrami, Philip C., and others. "Educational Seduction." *Review of Educational Research* 52 no. 3 (Fall 1982): 446-464.

Reports a meta-analysis of studies related to faculty evaluation and concludes that instructor expressiveness had a substantial impact on student ratings but a small impact on student achievement.

571. Abrami, Philip C., and others. *The Generalizability of Student Ratings of Instruction.* 1977. ERIC, ED 139 832.

Outlines the use of student ratings in the evaluation of faculty in higher education.

572. Abrami, Philip C., and others. "Multidimensionality of Student Ratings of Instruction." *Instructional Evaluation* 6 no. 1 (1981): 12-17.

Examines the multidimensional aspects of student ratings of instruction in higher education.

573. Abrami, Philip C., and others. "The Relationship Between Student Personality Characteristics, Teacher Ratings, and Student Achievement." *Journal of Education Psychology* 74 (1982): 111-125.

Reports on the relationship between student personality characteristics, teacher ratings, and student achievement and concludes that there are interactions between the variables studied.

574. Aleamoni, Lawrence M. "Some Practical Approaches for Faculty
       and Administrators." *New Directions for Teaching and Learning* 31
       (Fall 1987): 75-78.

       Suggests ways to develop comprehensive systems of
       instructional improvement and evaluation of higher education
       faculty.

575. Aleamoni, Lawrence M. "Student Ratings of Instruction." In
       Handbook of Teacher Evaluation, edited by Jason Millman, 110-
       145. Beverly Hills, CA: Sage Publications, 1981.

       Examines research on student ratings and presents a
       comprehensive system to improve and reward instructional
       effectiveness.

576. Aleamoni, Lawrence M. "Typical Faculty Concerns About Student
       Evaluation of Teaching." *New Directions for Teaching and
       Learning* 31 (Fall 1987): 25-31.

       Discusses eight of the most common faculty concerns about
       student evaluations of instruction including such factors as student
       judgment, perception that only colleagues are qualified to judge
       instruction, student-rating schemes as popularity contests, and
       reliability and validity.

577. Andreson, L. W., and others. "Competent Teaching and Its
       Appraisal." *Assessment and Evaluation in Higher Education* 12 no.
       1 (Spring 1987): 66-72.

       Presents the case that to judge faculty competence, the range of
       knowledge, skills, and attitudes constituting competence must be
       established, and that competence is composed of preparation for
       teaching, engagement in teaching, and professional development.

578. Arreola, Raoul A. *Essential Components of a Comprehensive
       Faculty Evaluation System.* 1979. ERIC, ED 176 604.

       Examines the development and validation of a comprehensive
       system for the evaluation of faculty in higher education.

579. Arubayi, Eric A. "Improvement of Instruction and Teacher Effectiveness: Are Student Ratings Reliable and Valid?" *Higher Education* 16 no. 3 (1987): 267-278.

    Reviews the literature and suggests a measure of consistency, stability, and validity of student ratings of teacher performance, with specific variables found to have a positive relationship with the ratings.

580. Bail, Frederick R., and others. *Student Evaluations of College Teaching.* 1979. ERIC, ED 180 357.

    Presents a 34-item student evaluation instrument designed to reliably measure major dimensions of college teaching effectiveness.

581. Berk, Ronald A. "The Construction of Rating Instruments for Faculty Evaluations: A Review of Methodological Issues." *Journal of Higher Education* 50 no. 5 (September/October 1979): 650-659.

    Reviews issues related to the construction of instruments for course and instructor evaluation by students.

582. Blackburn, R. T. and M. J. Clark. "An Assessment of Faculty Performance: Some Correlates Between Administrators, Colleagues, Students, and Self-ratings." *Sociology of Education* 48 no. 2 (1975): 242-256.

    Addresses the evaluation of faculty work performances and reviews conflicting studies of teaching and research.

583. Boice, Robert. "Reexamination of Traditional Emphases in Faculty Development." *Research in Higher Education* 21 no. 2 (1984): 195-209.

    Describes the use of clinically based direct interventions with colleagues to demonstrate ways of surmounting four constraints in faculty development research including the problems of engaging the least needy faculty, faculty who refuse feedback based on student ratings, improvement of teaching skills while making progress as writers, and teaching scholarly productivity.

584. Brandenburg, Dale C., and others. "Consideration for an Evaluation Process of Instructional Quality." *CEDR Quarterly* 12 no. 4 (Winter 1979): 8-12.

Describes five methods of faculty evaluation including questionnaires, written comments, group interviews, self-evaluations, and evaluation by peers.

585. Braskamp, L. A. and D. Caulley. *Student Rating and Instructor Self-ratings and Their Relationships to Student Achievement.* Urbana-Champaign, IL: University of Illinois, 1978.

Reviews student ratings and instructor self-ratings in relationship to student achievement in higher education classes.

586. Braxton, J. M., and A. M. Bayer. "Assessing Faculty Scholarly Performance." *New Directions for Institutional Research* 13 no. 2 (June 1986): 25-42.

Examines the measurement of faculty research performance and suggests the use of a variety of subjective and quantitative measures and weighting systems.

587. Brittingham, Barbara. "Faculty Development in Teacher Education: An Agenda." *Journal of Teacher Education* 37 no. 5 (September/October 1986): 2-5.

Proposes six priorities for faculty development which can strengthen the role of teacher education in the institution, while developing the vitality of the education faculty individually and collectively.

588. Cashin, William E. and Hugh M. Slawson. *IDEA Technical Reports No. 2.* Manhattan, KS: Center for Faculty Evaluation and Development in Higher Education, Kansas State University, 1977.

Describes the results of the development and field testing of the Instructional Development and Effective Assessment System (IDEA) for use in faculty evaluation.

589. Cashin, William E., and Hugh M. Slawson. *IDEA Technical Report No. 3*. Manhattan, KS: Center for Faculty Evaluation and Development in Higher Education, Kansas State University, 1977.

Describes additional results of the development and field testing of the Instructional Development and Effective Assessment System (IDEA) for use in faculty evaluation.

590. Cashin, William E., and Bruce E. Perrin. *IDEA Technical Report No. 4*. Manhattan, KS: Center for Faculty Evaluation and Development in Higher Education, Kansas State University, 1978.

Describes the data and computational procedures used by the Instructional Development and Effective Assessment System (IDEA) staff.

591. Centra, John A. "Colleagues as Raters of Classroom Instruction." *Journal of Higher Education* 46 no. 3 (1975): 327-338.

Discusses aspects of teaching and methods of assessing teaching that colleagues can judge.

592. Centra, John A. *Determining Faculty Effectiveness*. San Francisco: Jossey-Bass, 1979.

Summarizes research and approaches for assessing faculty and includes an examination of legal problems, and issues in research and scholarship, public service, and advising.

593. Centra, John A. "Formative and Summative Evaluation: Parody or Paradox?" *New Directions for Teaching and Learning* 31 (Fall 1987): 47-55.

Outlines six evaluation methods for faculty including student ratings, colleague evaluations, definitions of good teaching, teacher-designed examinations, evaluation of research and scholarship, and the politics of evaluation.

594. Centra, John A. *How Universities Evaluate Faculty Performance: A Survey of Department Heads.* 1977. ERIC, ED 157 445.

  Presents findings that the evaluation of research and scholarship of faculty in higher education depends very much on the level of the institution and type of department.

595. Centra, John A. "Self-ratings of College Teachers: A Comparison with Student Ratings." *Journal of Educational Psychology* 65 no. 3 (1973): 395-401.

  Examines college teachers' self-ratings and ratings given by students in order to compare instructional practices.

596. Centra, John A. "Student Ratings of Instruction and Their Relationship to Student Learning." *American Educational Research Journal* 14 no. 1 (Winter 1977): 17-24.

  Explores the relationship between student ratings of instruction and the amount of learning taking place as measured by course examination performance.

597. Centra, John A. "Types of Faculty Development Programs." *Journal of Higher Education* 49 no. 2 (1978): 151-162.

  Identifies four groups of faculty development practices including traditional practices, instructional assistance practices, assessment of faculty, and faculty improvement activities.

598. Centra, John A., and others. *Evaluating Teaching for Tenure and Promotion.* 1987. Syracuse, NY: Center for Instructional Development, Syracuse University.

  Outlines the steps needed to conduct a fair evaluation of college faculty for tenure and promotion considerations.

599. Claxton, Charles S., and Patricia H. Murrell. "Developmental Theory as a Guide for Maintaining the Validity of College Faculty." *New Directions for Teaching and Learning* 19 (September 1984): 29-44.

  Outlines Erikson's and Loevinger's theories of adult development and summarizes their application for college administrative practices in faculty evaluation, planning, tenure and promotion, and professional development.

600. Coburn, Louisa. *Student Evaluation of Teacher Performance.* 1984. ERIC, ED 289 887.

Summarizes the research on student evaluation of college teachers' performance and offers four arguments in favor of such evaluations, including: (1) students are the main source of information about the educational environment, (2) students are the most logical evaluators of student satisfactions, and effectiveness of the course; (3) the student-teacher communication involved raises the level of instruction; and (4) use of student ratings by other students in course selection may increase the possibilities that excellence in instruction will be rewarded.

601. Cohen, Peter A. "Effectiveness of Student Rating Feedback for Improving College Instruction: A Meta-analysis of Findings." *Research in Higher Education* 13 no. 4 (1980): 321-341.

Summarizes a meta-analysis of the effects of student feedback on the level of instruction.

602. Cohen, Peter A. "Student Ratings of Instruction and Student Achievement: A Meta-analysis of Multisection Validity Studies." *Review of Educational Research* 51 no. 3 (Fall 1981): 281-309.

Presents a summary of the use of meta-analysis to synthesize research on the relationship between student ratings of instruction and student achievement.

603. Creswell, John W. "Concluding Thoughts: Observing, Promoting, Evaluating, and Reviewing Research Performance." *New Directions for Institutional Research* 13 no. 2 (June 1986): 87-102.

Outlines the steps institutional personnel should use in assessing faculty research performance including: (1) the extent to which the institution rewards research; (2) ways to encourage faculty to be productive; (3) criteria for evaluating research performance; and (4) the specific steps useful in reviewing research performance within academic units.

604. DeNeve, Hubert M. F., and Piet J. Janssen. "Validity of Student Evaluation of Instruction." *Higher Education* 11 no. 5 (September 1982): 543-552.

Discusses a new questionnaire entitled "Evalec" (for evaluating faculty lecturing) which incorporates principles of both the appropriate teaching-learning model and the students' more subjective dimension.

605. Dienst, Evelyn R. *Evaluation By Colleagues.* 1981. ERIC, ED 209 341.

Describes a system for the peer evaluation of college faculty and reports the results from its implementation at one institution.

606. Donald, Janet G. "Quality Indices for Faculty Evaluation." *Assessment and Evaluation in Higher Education* 9 no. 1 (Spring 1984): 41-52.

Surveys the different indices in use for evaluating research, teaching, and service activities among faculty members.

607. Doyle, Kenneth O. "Development of the Student Opinion Survey." *Educational and Psychological Measurement* 37 no. 3 (1977): 439-443.

Describes the development and validation of the Student Opinion Survey designed to help in the evaluation of college faculty.

608. Doyle, Kenneth O. *Student Evaluation of Instruction.* Lexington, MA: Lexington Books, 1975.

Describes a system for using student evaluation to improve instruction in higher education.

609. Doyle, Kenneth O., and Patricia L. Webber. "Self Ratings of College Instruction." *American Educational Research Journal* 15 no. 3 (Summer 1978): 467-475.

Examines a correlational study of self-ratings of instruction with a variety of other ratings and concludes that the enjoyment of teaching and liking for the subject matter plays a major role in the instructor's definition of good teaching.

610. Echard, Pamela J. "Faculty Evaluation: The Basis for Rewards in Higher Education." *Peabody Journal of Education* 57 no. 2 (January 1980): 94-100.

Outlines the steps involved in evaluating college faculty including the decision making on the focus; evaluation design, criteria, data collection process, material review, and committee formation.

611. Elmore, Patricia B., and John T. Pohlmann. "An Automated Instructor Evaluation System." *AEDS Journal* 8 no. 4 (1975): 108-116.

Outlines the use of the Instructional Improvement Questionnaire as a means of evaluating and improving the quality of teaching of college faculty.

612. Elton, Lewis. "Evaluating Teaching and Assessing Teachers in Universities." *Assessment and Evaluation in Higher Education* 9 no. 2 (Summer 1984): 97-115.

Recounts the development of a model for faculty evaluation based on practices in other professions.

613. Erdle, S., and H. G. Murray. "Interfaculty Differences in Classroom Teaching Behaviors and Their Relationship to Student Instructional Ratings." *Research in Higher Education* 24 no. 3 (1986): 115-127.

Summarizes a study of 95 behaviors exhibited by 125 effective teachers as measured by end-of-term ratings averaged over a three year period.

614. Feldman, K. A. "Consistency and Variability Among College Students in Rating Their Teachers and Courses: A Review and Analysis." *Research in Higher Education* 6 no. 3 (1977): 233-274.

Explores whether student ratings are objective descriptions or subjective evaluative reactions to the faculty member.

615. Feldman, K. A. "Course Characteristics and College Students' Ratings of Their Teachers and Courses: What We Know and What We Don't." *Research in Higher Education* 6 no. 3 (1978): 199-242.

 Reviews course characteristics and the relationships to college students' ratings of the instructors.

616. Follman, John. *Student Ratings of Faculty Teaching Effectiveness: Revisited.* 1983. ERIC, ED 232 556.

 Reviews the literature from 1973 to 1983 on student ratings of faculty teaching effectiveness, explores myths and realities, and outlines several new instruments for rating faculty.

617. Gaff, Sally Shake, ed. *Resource Notebook* 1976. ERIC, ED 130 591.

 Provides a resource notebook related to all aspects of faculty development, evaluation, and renewal.

618. Galm, John A. "Welcome to Post-Tenure Review." *College Teaching* 33 no. 2 (Spring 1985): 65-67.

 Describes a series of post-tenure review seminars and the resulting professional renewal and improved peer relationships.

619. Garfield, E. *Citation Indexing: Its Theory and Application in Science, Technology, and Humanities.* New York: John Wiley and Sons, 1979.

 Outlines the use of the Citation Index as a measure of a faculty member's level of scholarship.

620. Genova, William J., and others. *Mutual Benefit Evaluation of Faculty and Administrators in Higher Education.* 1976. ERIC, ED 134 104.

 Discusses a practical guide for academic communities that are developing programs to evaluate faculty and administrators.

621. Gilmore, G. M., and others. "The Generalizability of Student Ratings of Instruction: Estimation of Teacher and Course Components." *Journal of Educational Measurement* 15 no. 1 (1978): 1-13.

Summarizes the use of ability theory to separate ratings of courses by students into various components and indicates reliable findings when generalizing over students and items and over students, items, and courses.

622. Greene, James E., and others. *Using Administrative Data as Unobtrusive Indicators of Teaching Performance*. 1983. ERIC, ED 232 590.

Investigates the use of unobtrusive indicators of teacher performance in order to address the issue of reliability and possible bias of students' evaluations.

623. Gunn, Bruce. "Evaluating Faculty Performance: A Holistic Approach." *Journal of the College and University Personnel Association* 34 no. 4 (Winter 1982): 23-30.

Describes a system of faculty evaluation that is based on a hierarchy of assessment stages including foundation (reviewing work goals, standards, and results), peer evaluation, self-assessment, administrator appraisal, and an arbitration committee.

624. Hauser, Jerald Allen. "A Study of Education-Department Member Satisfaction, Group Interaction, and Work-Attitude: Comparisons and Profile Stability." Ph.D. dissertation, Marquette University, 1978.

Examines profiles of program satisfaction, interaction, and work attitudes that are exhibited by the membership of three teacher-preparation programs.

625. Ho, May Lein. "Competencies of Curriculum Materials Center Directors in Teacher-Education Institutions." Ed.D. dissertation, East Texas State University, 1984.

Analyzes essential skills for individuals who serve as directors of materials centers in teacher education institutions.

626. Horine, Larry. "Faculty Performance Evaluation: One Answer to Accountability Demands." *Journal of Physical Education and Recreation* 52 no. 7 (September 1981): 78-79.

Outlines an instrument to measure nonteaching performance in a department of physical education.

627. Hoyt, Donald P., and William E. Cashin. *IDEA Technical Report No. 1.* Manhattan, KS: Center for Faculty Evaluation and Development in Higher Education, Kansas State University, 1977.

Describes the development of the Instructional Development and Effective Assessment System (IDEA) for use in faculty evaluation.

628. Joint Committee on Standards for Educational Evaluation. *The Personnel Evaluation Standards: How to Assess Systems for Evaluating Educators.* Newberry Park, CA: Sage Publications, Inc., 1988.

Examines the evaluation of educational personnel at all levels.

629. Kronk, Annie K., and Thomas A. Shipka. *Evaluation of Faculty in Higher Education: A Handbook for Faculty Leaders.* 1980. ERIC, ED 217 783.

Includes consideration of aspects of evaluation that directly effect employee decisions of faculty and faculty leaders.

630. Lacefield, Warren E. "Faculty Enrichment and the Assessment of Teaching." *Review of Higher Education* 9 no. 4 (1986): 361-379.

Describes the use of Faculty Enrichment and Assessment of Teaching, a process-oriented method of student evaluation of instruction developed specifically for use in health education programs.

631. Leventhal, Les, and others. *Bogus Evidence for the Validity of Student Ratings.* 1977. ERIC, ED 150 510.

Examines evidence for the validity of student ratings of faculty in higher eduction.

632. Leventhal, Les, and others. "Educational Seduction and the Validity of Student Ratings." *Improving University Teaching* 5 (1979): 373-382.

Examines the validity of student ratings in evaluating higher education faculty.

633. Licata, Christine M. *Post-Tenure Faculty Evaluation: Threat or Opportunity?* 1986. ERIC, ED 270 009.

Outlines the factors that have led to post-tenure evaluation of faculty along with limitations of tenure and current post-tenure evaluation practices.

634. Lichty, Richard W., and Jerrold M. Peterson. *Peer Evaluations--A Necessary Part of Evaluating Teaching Effectiveness.* 1979. ERIC, ED 175 352.

Explains peer evaluation in assessing teaching effectiveness and outlines two methods of conducting such evaluations.

635. Lin, Y., and others. "The Use of Ratings in Promotion Decisions." *Journal of Higher Education* 55 no. 5 (1984): 583-589.

Finds that direct quotations from student ratings of teachers are more persuasive than statistical summaries of ratings in evaluating teaching ability for promotion decisions.

636. Lyons, P. R. *Program Evaluation of Graduate Education.* 1979. ERIC, ED 174 176.

Includes a discussion of graduate level education program evaluation emphasizing faculty evaluation by students.

637. Marlin, James W. "Student Perception of End-of-Course Evaluations." *Journal of Higher Education* 58 no. 6 (November/December 1987): 704-716.

Reports the results of a survey of students who consider themselves fair and accurate in evaluating faculty but do not understand the use and effects of the ratings and believe that neither faculty nor administrators pay any attention to the results.

638. Marsh, Herbert W. "Students' Evaluations of University Teaching: Dimensionality, Reliability, Validity, Potential Biases, and Utility." *Journal of Educational Psychology* 76 no.5 (October 1984): 707-754.

    Reviews findings and research designs used to study university students' evaluations to teaching effectiveness and describes a construct validation approach which recognizes the multidimensionality of both effective teaching and students' evaluations.

639. Marsh, Herbert W. "Students' Evaluations of University Teaching: Research Findings, Methodological Issues, and Directions for Future Research." *International Journal of Educational Research* 11 no. 3 (1987): 253-388.

    Summarizes a meta-analysis on student evaluations of college teaching and concludes they are multidimensional, reliable, valid, and relatively unbiased.

640. Marsh, Herbert W. "Validity of Students' Evaluations of College Teaching: A Multitrait-Multimethod Analysis." *Journal of Educational Psychology* 74 no. 2 (1982): 264-279.

    Summarizes a study of teaching effectiveness based on student ratings of undergraduate and graduate courses and multifactor rating scales.

641. Marsh, H. W., and others. "Validity of Student Evaluations of Instructional Effectiveness: A Comparison of Faculty Self-Evaluations by Their Students." *Educational Psychology* 71 no. 2 (1979): 149-160.

    Discusses a comparison of student evaluations of faculty and faculty self-evaluations and concludes the two groups were measuring the same basic traits.

642. Marsh, Herbert W., and J. U. Overall. "Validity of Students'
Evaluations of Teaching Effectiveness: Cognitive and Affective
Criteria." *Journal of Educational Psychology* 72 (1980): 468-475.

Examines the validity of student evaluations of teaching
effectiveness of higher education faculty taking into account both
cognitive and affective criteria.

643. Marsh, Herbert W., and J. E. Ware. "Effects of Expressiveness,
Content Coverage, and Incentive on Multidimensional Student
Rating Scales: New Interpretations of the Dr. Fox Effect." *Journal
of Educational Psychology* 74 no. 1 (1982): 126-134.

Reports a study of the effects of expressiveness and content
coverage on student achievement and evaluation in college courses.

644. McKeachie, W. J. "Can Evaluating Instruction Improve
Teaching?" *New Directions for Teaching and Learning* 31 (Fall
1987): 3-7.

Reports that evaluation alone will probably not improve
teaching, but when it is accompanied by feedback, information
about teaching and learning, and work within knowledgeable
consultant, evaluation may lead to improvement.

645. McKnight, Phil. *Beyond the Questionnaires and the Data:
Developing a Model of Faculty Evaluation.* 1986. ERIC, ED 274
718.

Discusses issues concerning students' evaluation of college
faculty, including the identification of relevant variables or
paradigms and the models and theories used to establish
relationships between the variables.

646. McLean, James E. *A Useful University Departmental Evaluation
System.* 1987. ERIC, ED 296 661.

Describes a faculty evaluation plan based on four principles:
broad-based faculty and administrative support; informing faculty of
expectations prior to evaluations; describing the primary decision-
making and data-gathering roles played by students, faculty, and
administration; and providing feedback and resources to assist

faculty in enhancing their performance and achieving their career goals.

647. Meyer, D. Eugene, and Charles W. Smith. "A Nationwide Survey of Teacher Education Faculty Evaluation Practices." *College Student Journal Monograph* 11 no. 1 (1977): 1-16.

   Summarizes the results of a nationwide survey of factors related to faculty such as student evaluations, teaching effectiveness, salary scales, merit pay plan, and tenure and promotion factors.

648. Miller, Allen H. "Student Assessment of Teaching in Higher Education." *Higher Education* 17 no. 1 (1988): 3-15.

   Issues in the debate over student evaluations of college faculty are discussed, including appropriate measures of teaching effectiveness, reasons for assessing teaching, reliability and validity of student ratings, and how assessments are conducted.

649. Miller, R. I. *Evaluating Faculty for Promotion and Tenure.* San Francisco: Jossey-Bass, 1985.

   Outlines systems and ways of evaluating faculty for promotion and tenure and also provides an extensive review of the literature.

650. Murray, Harry G. "Acquiring Student Feedback That Improves Instruction." *New Directions for Teaching and Learning* 32 (Winter 1987): 85-96.

   Discusses formative evaluation of teaching and ways of obtaining diagnostic feedback that will lead to improved teaching in large lecture classes.

651. Murray, Harry G. "Classroom Teaching Behaviors Related to College Teaching Effectiveness." *New Directions for Teaching and Learning* 23 (1985): 21-34.

   Looks at the behaviors of college faculty in the classroom and describes feedback and training procedures designed to modify inappropriate behaviors.

652. Naftulin, D. H., and others. "The Doctor Fox Lecture: A Paradigm of Education Seduction." *Journal of Medical Education* 48 no. 7 (1973): 630-635.

    Presents results of a questionnaire that indicate that educators must evaluate their effectiveness beyond the satisfaction with which their students view them.

653. Newton, Robert R. "Performance Evaluation in Education." *Journal of the College and University Personnel Association* 33 no. 2 (1982): 39-43.

    Presents a system for faculty evaluation that suggests a performance middle ground appropriate to the realities of teaching while promoting the values associated with performance-based evaluation.

654. O'Hanlon, James, and Lynn Mortensen. "Making Teacher Evaluation Work." *Journal of Higher Education* 51 no. 6 (November/December 1980): 664-672.

    Looks at five approaches to the evaluation of teaching that can help improve instruction and making administrative decisions about pay, rank, and tenure.

655. Orban, Deborah A., and Allan J. Abedor. "Organizational Change and the Development of Faculty Evaluation Systems." *Journal of Instructional Development* 8 no. 1 (1985): 22-25.

    Describes problems in faculty evaluation and performance appraisal and some assumptions and features of newer alternative faculty evaluation systems.

656. Ory, John C., and Larry A. Braskamp. "Faculty Perceptions of the Quality and Usefulness of Three Types of Evaluative Information. *Research in Higher Education* 15 no. 3 (1981): 271-282.

    Investigates faculty perceptions of student evaluative information collected by three methods, including objective questionnaire items, open-ended questions, and group interviews.

657. Parramore, Barbara M. "Evaluation of University Faculty."
     CEDR Quarterly 12 no. 4 (Winter 1979): 3-7.

     Describes and summarizes the use of a set of faculty evaluation
     guidelines for five years at one institution of higher education.

658. Perry, Raymond P., and others. "Educational Seduction: The
     Effects of Instructor Expressiveness and Lecture Content on Student
     Ratings and Achievement." *Journal of Educational Psychology* 71
     (1979): 107-116.

     Looks at the relationships between student ratings and
     achievement and the expressiveness of the instructor and the content
     of the lectures.

659. Purcell, Larry O. *Factors Affecting the Quality of Staff
     Development.* 1987. ERIC, ED 285 862.

     Reviews the quality and effectiveness of faculty and staff
     development activities as they relate to improving teaching
     performance.

660. Riegle, Rodney P., and Dent M. Rhodes. "Avoiding Mixed
     Metaphors of Faculty Evaluation." *College Teaching* 34 no. 4
     (Fall 1986): 123-128.

     Discusses five metaphors of faculty evaluation including
     judging, criticizing, assessing, appraising, and rating.

661. Root, L. "Faculty Evaluation: Reliability of Peer Assessments of
     Research, Teaching, and Service." *Research in Higher Education* 26
     no. 1 (1987): 71-84.

     Analyzes the assessments of faculty performance for the purpose
     of determining salary increases.

662. Rutherford, Desmond. "Indicators of Performance: Some Practical
     Suggestions." *Assessment and Evaluation in Higher Education* 12
     no. 1 (Spring 1987): 46-55.

     Explores indicators for use in monitoring individual and
     departmental performance in teaching and research.

663. Saaty, Thomas L., and Vasudevan Ramanujam. "An Objective Approach to Faculty Promotion and Tenure by the Analytical Hierarchy Process." *Research in Higher Education* 18 no. 3 (1983): 311-331.

Explains and illustrates a faculty evaluation system that classifies factors within a hierarchy and weights each, producing a final composite set for each faculty member.

664. Salthouse, T. A., and others. "An Experimental Investigation of Factors Affecting University Promotions Decision." *Journal of Higher Education* 49 no. 2 (1978): 177-183.

Summarizes the results of a study in which student ratings were used as a major factor in university promotion decisions.

665. Seibert, Warren F. *Elevating the Importance of Teaching.* 1977. ERIC, ED 161 312.

Outlines the development and validation of the Purdue "CAFETERIA" system for faculty evaluation.

666. Seldin, Peter. "Evaluating College Teaching." *New Directions for Teaching and Learning* 33 (Spring 1988): 47-56.

Summaries a decade of research on the evaluation of college teaching and indicates that a wide variety of approaches and a concise set of practical guidelines for assisting college teachers in improving their teaching has been developed.

667. Seldin, Peter. "Evaluating Teaching Performance: Answers to Common Questions." *AGB Reports* 30 no. 1 (January/February 1988): 34-39.

Answers commonly asked questions about methods of faculty evaluation (including student, peer, and self-evaluation) and offers guidelines for improving a failing evaluation system.

668. Seldin, Peter. *Successful Faculty Evaluation Programs. A Practical Guide to Improve Faculty Performance and Promotion/Tenure Decisions.* Crugers, NY: Coventry Press, 1980.

    Discusses seven separate areas of faculty evaluation—student colleague and self-assessment; student learning; student advising; institutional service, research, and publication--and provides suggestions for establishing a faculty evaluation program.

669. Sheehan, D. S. "On the Invalidity of Student Ratings for Administrative Personnel Decisions." *Journal of Higher Education* 46 (1975): 687-700.

    Questions the validity of using student ratings of instructional effectiveness for making personnel decisions.

670. Soderberg, L. O. "Dominance of Research and Publication: An Unrelenting Tyranny." *College Teaching* 33 no. 4 (Fall 1985): 168-172.

    Examines the role of publishing and research in the evaluation process for higher education faculty.

671. Stevens, Joseph J. "Additional Sources and Information." *New Directions for Teaching and Learning* 31 (Fall 1987): 83-91.

    Presents an annotated bibliography on instructional evaluation and improvement in higher education with emphasis on uncommon techniques.

672. Stevens, Joseph J. "Using Student Ratings to Improve Instruction." *New Directions for Teaching and Learning* 31 (Fall 1987): 33-38.

    Indicates that if instructional improvement programs are likely to be effective, in addition to providing feedback to instructors, there is a need for a system to provide institutional support, reward, and training.

673. Sullivan, A. M., and G. R. Skanes. "Validity of Student Evaluation of Teaching and Characteristics of Successful Instructors." *Journal of Educational Psychology* 66 no. 4 (1974): 84-90.

    Reports a study of the relationship between student ratings of instructors and characteristics of highly rated instructors.

674. Tapsuwan, Suda. "Assessment of the Roles and Functions of Graduate Advisors in a School of Education." Ph.D. dissertation, Oregon State University, 1984.

    Reports the determination and assessment of the roles and functions of graduate advisors and provides constructive feedback to graduate advisors.

675. Tracey, Richard. *Now Make the Most of Your Student Ratings.* 1985. ERIC, ED 289 434.

    Outlines ways to interpret data from student ratings of teacher performance and to maximumize the use of student ratings.

676. Wallace, Patricia M. "Performance Evaluation: The Use of a Single Instrument for University Librarians and Teaching Faculty." *Journal of Academic Librarianship* 12 no. 5 (November 1986): 284-290.

    Describes an instrument that can be used for evaluating the performance of both university librarians and teaching faculty.

677. Ware, John E., and Reed G. Williams. "Discriminant Analysis of Student Ratings as a Means of Identifying Lecturers Who Differ in Enthusiasm or Information Giving." *Educational and Psychological Measurement* 37 no. 4 (1977): 627-639.

    Investigates the use of discriminate analysis in identifying faculty members who differ in enthusiasm and/or information giving.

678. Weimer, Maryellen Gleason. "Translating Evaluation Results into Teaching Improvements." *AAHE Bulletin* 39 no. 8 (April 1987). Full text contained in ERIC, ED 283 444.

Outlines five problems concerning faculty evaluations: (1) summative and formative evaluation objectives are mixed; (2) most instructional evaluation is designed with institutional convenience in mind; (3) evaluation results are given impersonally; (4) most instruments have not been empirically evaluated; and (5) evaluation results look precise, objective, and meaningful.

679. Welch, Betty Jo. "MBO: Faculty Evaluation and Development." *ACA Bulletin* 56 (April 1986): 14-18.

Examines a faculty development program that is based on management by objectives.

680. Williams, Reed G., and John E. Ware. "An Extended Visit With Dr. Fox: Validity of Student Ratings of Instruction After Repeated Exposures to a Lecturer." *American Educational Research Journal* 14 no. 4 (Fall 1977): 449-457.

Compares the types of lectures that students prefer and the level of achievement under each condition.

681. Williams, Reed G., and John E. Ware. "Validity of Student Ratings of Instruction Under Different Incentive Conditions: A Further Study of the Dr. Fox Effect." *Journal of Educational Psychology* 68 (1976): 48-56.

Examines the validity of student ratings of instruction under different incentive conditions.

682. Wilson, Robert C. "Toward Excellence in Teaching." *New Directions for Teaching and Learning* 31 (Fall 1987): 9-24.

Summarizes a study of student evaluations of teaching and getting the faculty to accept specific suggestions and put them into practice.

683. Wotruba, T. R., and P. L. Wright. "How to Develop a Teacher-Rating Instrument: A Research Approach." *Journal of Higher Education* 46 no. 6 (1975): 653-663.

Introduces a five step methodology for developing and implementing a teaching effectiveness rating instrument.

Physical Facilities

684. ACRL. "Administrator's Checklist of Microcomputer Concerns in Education Libraries." *College and Research Libraries News* (January 1986): 69-71.

Provides a checklist to be used in evaluating microcomputers for use in education libraries.

685. ACRL. "Guidelines for Extended Campus Library Services." *College and Research Libraries News* (March 1982): 86-88.

Summarizes some of the guidelines that should be considered in providing library services to off-campus locations and in extension programs.

686. ACRL. "The Mission of a University Undergraduate Library: Model Statement." *College and Research Libraries News* (October 1987): 542-544.

Summarizes standards for evaluating the undergraduate library.

687. ACRL. "Model Statement of Objectives for Academic Bibliographic Instruction: Draft Revision." *College and Research Libraries News* (May 1987): 256-261.

Provides a checklist for evaluation of the academic bibliographic instruction that occurs within a library program.

688. Anderson, Cheryl A. "Computer Literacy: Changes for Teacher Education." *Journal of Teacher Education* 34 no. 5 (September/October 1983): 6-9.

Examines the need for training preservice and inservice teachers in computer literacy and analyzes the need for computing facilities in schools, colleges, and departments of education.

689. Association of Physical Plant Administrators of Universities and Colleges. *Professionals Working Together.* 1985. ERIC, ED 264 775.

Includes an extensive section on the evaluation of physical facilities in higher education.

690. Burns, Josh, and others. *The College and University Energy Management Workbook.* 1984. ERIC, ED 251 041.

Reviews an energy management workbook for use by colleges and universities.

691. Castaldi, B. *Educational Facilities: Planning, Modernization, and Management.* Boston: Allyn and Bacon, Inc., 1987.

Discusses all types of educational facilities and provides various methods for their evaluation.

692. Christiansen, Dorothy E., and others. "Guide to Collection Evaluation Through Use and User Studies." *Library Resources and Technical Services* (October/December 1983): 432-440.

Suggests strategies for the evaluation of library collections in various academic areas.

693. Council of Educational Facility Planners. *Space Planning Guidelines.* 1985. ERIC, ED 298 611.

Examines planning guidelines to be used as aids in determining needs for the allocation and reallocation of existing and new space in educational facilities.

694. Englehardt, David F. "The Role of Facility Planners in Controlling Costs of Educational Facilities." *CEFP Journal* 22 no. 6 (November/December 1984): 18-21.

Explores the use of facility planners in the pre-bid and preconstruction phases for new structures.

695. Eubanks, David L. "School Facility Evaluation: Physical Plant and Instructional Program--Do They Work Together?" *School Business Affairs* 51 no. 1 (January 1985): 22.

Reports criteria and methods for periodically evaluating and determining the adequacy of education facilities.

696. Foldsey, G. *A Paradigm for Teacher Involvement in the Development of Educational Specifications.* 1985. ERIC, ED 267 021.

Includes ways of involving the faculty in the development of specifications for educational facilities.

697. Glass, T. E. "Educational Specifications: A Blueprint for the Future Program." *CEFP Journal* 24 no. 1 (1984): 4-13.

Looks at educational specifications and their use in the design and development of educational facilities.

698. Haka, Clifford H., and Nancy Stevens. *A Guidebook for Shelf Inventory Procedures in Academic Libraries.* Washington: Association of Research Libraries, 1985.

Examines the procedures for conducting shelf inventories in academic libraries.

699. Hawkins, Harold L. *Appraisal Guide for School Facilities.* Midland, MI: Pendell Publishing Company, 1977.

Presents an instrument for use in measuring the quality of school facilities in such areas as site, structural and mechanical features, building environment, school safety, space utilization, and maintainability.

700. Hawkins, Harold L., and H. Edward Lilley. *Guide for School Facility Appraisal.* Columbus, OH: Council for Educational Facility Planners, 1986.

    Provides evaluative criteria for the elementary-secondary administrator to use in measuring the quality of a school's facilities for general condition and suitability for education programs and has application in the evaluation of facilities for the preparation of teachers.

701. Heller, Paul, and Betsey Brenneman. "A Checklist for Evaluating Your Library's Handbook." *College and Research Libraries News* (February 1988): 78-80.

    Lists various elements that should be considered in the evaluation of a library handbook.

702. Hill, John C. "Performance-Based Evaluation of Educational Facilities." *CEFP Journal* 22 no. 2 (March/April 1984): 8-12.

    Looks at performance-based evaluation, along with a database of reliable and objective information concerning existing educational facilities, as an aid for planners in identifying facility needs.

703. Hollowood, James R. "Designing Microcomputer Facilities for Continuing Education." *New Directions for Continuing Education* 29 (March 1986): 17-27.

    Discusses several elements to consider in the establishment of the computer laboratory and offers guidelines for creating a microcomputer facility to meet specific needs.

704. Indiana State Advisory Council on Vocational Education. *School Building/Site Assessment Packet for Vocational Education Facilities: Instruction Manual.* 1978. ERIC, ED 171 912.

    Provides an assessment package for determining the suitability of structures for use in vocational and other educational facilities.

705. Kaiser, Harvey H., ed. "Planning and Managing Higher Education Facilities." *New Directions for Institutional Research* 61 (1989): 1-107.

    Includes a series of essays on the management of campus physical resources specifically designed for institutional researchers and others involved in planning and management of specific programs.

706. King, Jonathan. "Evaluation: A Firm Undertakes Re-examination of Its Work from the Users' Viewpoints." *AIA Journal* 65 no. 8 (1976): 29-30.

    Describes the approach taken by a large architectural firm toward gathering feedback on user satisfaction with educational facilities designed by the firm.

707. Lilley, H. E. "Computerizing Educational Specifications." *CEFP Journal* 23 no. 1 (1985): 14-16.

    Summarizes a method for computerizing educational specifications for use in facilities design.

708. Mosher, Paul H., and Marcia Pankake. "A Guide to Coordinated and Cooperative Collection Development." *Library Resources and Technical Services* (October/December 1983): 432-440.

    Offers suggestions and standards for the development and evaluation of library collections.

709. Mosmann, Charles. *Criteria for Instructional Computing Evaluation in Higher Education.* 1976. ERIC, ED 124 194.

    Describes a methodology for the evaluation of computer services for instructional purposes in higher education.

710. Muller, Kris, and others. "Space Planning Guidelines for Institutions of Higher Education." *CEFP Journal* 23 no. 5 (September/October 1985): 15-17.

    Gives examples of space guidelines designed so that an institution can select planning modules for the allocation of space as well as for the acquisition and construction of new space.

711. Nelson, Norbert J., and others. *Instruments and Procedures for Evaluating and Assessing the Status of Vocational Education Facilities in Indiana.* 1978. ERIC, ED 171 911.

Presents instruments and procedures for the evaluation of vocational education facilities that have application to the evaluation of higher education.

712. New Jersey State Department of Education. *School Facilities Evaluation Instrument. Education Facility Series. A Guide to Planning.* 1976. ERIC, ED 130 389.

Reviews the use of a school facilities evaluation instrument used in New Jersey.

713. Nutter, Norma. *Resources Needed for an Excellent Teacher Preparation Program.* 1984. ERIC, ED 250 298.

Summarizes the resources needed for the implementation of a teacher preparation program.

714. Piele, Philip, and Darrell Wright. *Evaluating the Existing School Plant.* 1976. ERIC, ED 117 783.

Provides guidelines for evaluating existing school buildings and lists the various elements of the building and its properties.

715. Sales, Gregory C. "Design Considerations for Planning a Computer Classroom." *Educational Technology* 25 no. 5 (May 1985): 7-13.

Discusses issues to be considered in setting up an efficient computer classroom, including selection, preparation, and furnishing of facilities.

716. Schlofeldt, J. "Telecommunications and Computer Requirements in the Development of Educational Specifications." *CEFP Journal* 24 no. 1 (1986): 21-23.

Reviews the telecommunications and computer requirements in the development of educational specifications for teacher education programs.

717. Stewart, G. Kent. "The Capital Resources Maintenance Audit."
     CEFP Journal 22 no. 3 (May/June 1984): 9-11.

     Lists eleven categories of data that are needed for conducting an
     audit of capital resources.

718. Toper, Richard P. "Save that College Building." *AGB Reports* 18
     no. 1 (1976): 14-17.

     Describes a system for analyzing buildings and making
     renovations, remodeling, and recycling for better utilization.

719. Wentling, Tim L., and William E. Piland. *Evaluating Facilities.*
     1982. ERIC, ED 225 024.

     Discusses various systems for the evaluation of facilities that are
     applicable in elementary and secondary schools and in higher
     education facilities.

720. Wiley, A. L. *Building Design and the Architect: An Instructional
     Module.* 1982. ERIC, ED 252 191.

     Lists seven areas of facilities planning that should be considered,
     including activities to be housed in the facility, people involved,
     furniture and equipment, program implementation, time of use of
     areas, preference of staff for teaching methods and materials, and
     curriculum emphasis.

Financial Analysis

721. Adams, Carl R. "Appraising Information Needs of Decision
     Makers." *New Directions for Institutional Research* 15 (1977): 1-
     78.

     Reports the results of several studies related to the information
     needs of higher education administrators in the decision-making
     process.

722. Allbright, A. Rodney. "Institutional Planning and Budgeting--A Team Approach." *Community College Review* 7 (1979): 30-35.

   Analyzes the planning and management systems that are in place in higher education and makes suggestions for improving the processes.

723. Balderston, Frederick E. "Note on Professor Sizer's Paper." *International Journal of Institutional Management in Higher Education* 3 no. 1 (May 1979): 76-77.

   Examines issues suggested by John Sizer's paper, "An Overview of the Assessment of Institutional Performance," including the efficient-frontier approach, multiple-criterion decision-making models, performance analysis approaches such as path analysis, and assessment of academic quality.

724. Berdahl, Robert O. "Legislative Program Evaluation." *New Directions for Institutional Research* 16 (1977): 35-66.

   Illustrates processes and effects of state performance audits of higher education programs (including education) in Wisconsin and Virginia.

725. Bowen, Howard R. "Cost Differences: The Amazing Disparity Among Institutions of Higher Education and Educational Costs Per Student." *Change* 13 no. 1 (1981): 21-27.

   Investigates differences among institutions in costs per student and raises questions about the manner in which higher education is financed for different types of programs.

726. Bowen, Howard R. "The Products of Higher Education." *New Directions for Institutional Research* 1 (1974): 1-22.

   Discusses the steps in attaining institutional accountability through goal definition, ordering priorities, identifying and measuring outcomes, comparing goals and outcomes, determining the degree to which the goals are being achieved, and measuring the cost.

727. Brinkman, Paul T. "Factors Affecting Instructional Costs at Major Research Universities." *Journal of Higher Education* 52 (1981): 265-279.

Assesses, through the use of regression analysis, instructional costs at major research institutions and concludes that much of the variation can be accounted for in terms of institutional differences and instructional output.

728. Bush, Robert N. "Education Reform: Lessons from the Past Half Century." *Journal of Teacher Education* 38 no. 3 (1987): 13-19.

Summarizes the reform efforts in teacher education for the past half century and asserts that teacher education has not received adequate funding when compared with other fields of study.

729. Cherrington, B. E. "Cost Analysis in Academic Decision Making." *Educational Record* 60 no. 2 (Spring 1979): 185-196.

Summarizes various cost analysis techniques and discusses the role of the dean, department chair, and senior administrators in the process.

730. Denton, Jon J., and Nick L. Smith. *A Cost Effectiveness Evaluation in Teacher Education.* 1984. ERIC, ED 253 513.

Explores the costs associated with the operation of teacher education programs and provides suggestions for integration of the information into the decision making process.

731. Denton, Jon J., and Nick L. Smith. *A Cost Effectiveness Evaluation of Alternate Secondary Level Teacher Preparation Programs.* 1984. ERIC, ED 242 725.

Examines the cost effectiveness of two alternative programs for the preparation of individuals seeking entry into the profession as secondary teachers and includes a discussion of the differences in the two programs.

732. Dickmeyer, Nathan, and K. Scott Hughes. *Financial Self-Assessment: A Workbook for Colleges.* 1980. ERIC, ED 198 753.

     Describes a simplified system for financial self-assessment that is applicable to the evaluation of teacher education programs.

733. Dickmeyer, Nathan, and K. Scott Hughes. *Self-Assessment of Financial Condition. A Preliminary Edition of a Workbook for Small Independent Institutions.* 1979. ERIC, ED 175 322.

     Describes a simple method for the self-assessment of the financial condition of small independent colleges with application to programs for the preparation of teachers.

734. Dressel, Paul, and Lou A. Simon. "Allocating Resources Among Departments." *New Directions for Institutional Research* 11 (1976): 1-76.

     Presents a series of essays that reflect an attempt by one institution to develop a budgeting process for incorporating the allocation of financial resources to departments.

735. Dunn, John W. "Financially Autonomous Colleges in a Multi-College System." *Community and Junior College Journal* 45 no. 7 (1975): 10-11.

     Reviews the use of formula budgeting in solving the problems of financing multi-college institutions, including programs for the preparation of teachers.

736. Frazer, Jeanette L., and Barbara W. Wright. "Program Organization." *New Directions for Institutional Research* 17 (1978): 41-51.

     Indicates that, to have policy relevance, a cost-per-student amount must analyze the education output units, be comparable across educational programs, and provide sufficient information for decision making.

737. Gifford, Bernard R. "A Commentary on Hawley." *American Journal of Education* 95 no. 2 (1987): 304-308.

Critiques the position that extended teacher preparation programs are likely to reduce the quality and quantity of teachers and that the position is entirely driven by cost considerations.

738. Gonyea, Meredith A., ed. "Analyzing and Constructing Costs." *New Directions for Institutional Research* 17 (1978).

Discusses strategies for applying the methods of cost analysis to programs in higher education.

739. Hawley, Willis D. "The High Costs and Doubtful Efficacy of Extended Teacher-Preparation Programs: An Invitation to More Basic Reforms." *American Journal of Education* 95 no. 2 (February 1987): 275-298.

Indicates that extended teacher education programs are likely to increase costs, reduce the quality and quantity of teachers, and will not improve teacher performance.

740. Hines, Edward R., and John R. McCarthy. *Higher Education Finance.* New York: Garland Publishing, 1984.

Includes annotated references to higher education finance that may be of use in evaluating a teacher education program.

741. Manning, M. L., and Kevin L. Swick. "Revitalizing Teacher Education: Fiscal and Program Concerns." *Action in Teacher Education* 6 no. 3 (1984): 76-79.

Outlines concerns relative to the fiscal support being provided for teacher education programs and makes suggestions for needed changes.

742. Monahan, William G., and others. *Fiscal Conditions and Implications in Selected Schools and Colleges of Education in Comprehensive Universities, 1982-83.* 1984. ERIC, ED 234 046.

Investigates the fiscal condition of schools and colleges of education in comprehensive universities and makes recommendations for changes in funding.

743. Norris, Robert G. *Analyzing the Cost Efficiency of Academic Departments and Instructional Personnel at State Universities.* 1981. ERIC, ED 208 709.

     Presents a cost-effectiveness model for academic administrators to use in making evaluation and planning decisions related directly to the instructional activities of academic departments.

744. Olagunju, Amos O. *MIS/TIS/IR Seven-Year, Long-Range Plan: Developed to Substantiate a Request for Title III SDIP Funds.* ERIC, ED 224 386.

     Summarizes a master long-range plan for a teacher education program that was developed to substantiate a request for financial assistance for strengthening developing institutions.

745. Orr, P. G., and Bruce A. Peseau. "Formula Funding is Not the Problem in Teacher Education." *Peabody Journal of Education* 57 (1979): 61-71.

     Analyzes some of the problems relative to the funding of programs for the preparation of teachers.

746. Peseau, Bruce A. "Developing an Adequate Resource Base for Teacher Education." *Journal of Teacher Education* 33 no. 4 (1982): 13-15.

     Outlines the steps needed to establish an adequate resource base to support teacher education programs.

747. Peseau, Bruce A. *Resources Allocated to Teacher Education in State Universities and Land-Grant Colleges.* 1984. ERIC, ED 250 297.

     Reports data concerning the funding and productivity of teacher education divisions in major state universities and land-grant colleges in the United States.

748. Peseau, Bruce A., and others. "A Cost Model for Clinical Teacher Education." *Action in Teacher Education* 9 no. 1 (Spring 1987): 21-34.

   Describes activities for the clinical preparation of teachers, provides actual cost data from eight teacher preparation programs, and presents a cost model for clinical experiences.

749. Peseau, Bruce A., and P. G. Orr. "The Outrageous Underfunding of Teacher Education." *Phi Delta Kappan* 62 no. 2 (October 1980): 100-102.

   Examines the problems associated with the apparent underfunding of teacher education programs.

750. Riley, Eric. "Marketing Policy and Its Cost in a College of Higher Education." *Educational Management and Administration* 12 no. 3 (Autumn 1984): 217-225.

   Discusses the development of advertising and publicity strategies and policy for student recruitment at a college of education.

751. Robinson, Daniel D. *Analysis and Interpretation of Financial Data.* 1975. ERIC, ED 114 001.

   Offers suggestions for understanding and using financial reports for improving programs for the preparation of teachers.

752. St. John, Edward P. "Management System Development: An Intervention Model for Developing Colleges and Universities." *Journal of Higher Education* 51 (1980): 285-300.

   Describes a suggested management model that provides for viewing the relationships between the structural characteristics of an institution and the types of management systems that should be employed.

753. St. John, Edward P. "Planning for Improved Management." *New Directions for Institutional Research* 31 (1981): 71-83.

   Reviews the needs for and ways of conducting needs assessments for use in designing the most appropriate management systems for teacher and other professional preparation programs.

754. Sassone, P. G., and W. A. Schaffer. *Cost-Benefit Analysis: A Handbook*. New York: Academic Press, 1978.

Describes cost-benefit analysis in higher education with applications to specific types of programs.

755. Schroeder, Roger G. "Management System Design: A Critical Approach." *New Directions for Institutional Research* 13 (1977): 99-114.

Describes the development of improved management systems for colleges and universities through the use of correct assumptions and a well-defined process.

756. Schroder, Roger G. "A Survey of Management Science in University Operations." *Management Science* 19 (1973): 895-906.

Discusses the applications and research of the management sciences in institutions of higher education, including planning, programming, and budget systems; management information systems; resource allocation models; and mathematical models.

757. Seldin, Clement A. "Off-Campus Inservice Activities: A Status Report." *Educational Research Quarterly* 7 no. 2 (Summer 1982): 31-41.

Summarizes a study of the off-campus activities of schools, colleges, and departments located in institutions that are members of the National Association of State Universities and Land Grant Colleges.

758. Sizer, John. "Assessing Institutional Performance--An Overview." *International Journal of Institutional Management in Higher Education* 3 no. 1 (May 1979): 49-75.

Addresses assessment of performance in institutions of higher education and the development of performance indicators including cost factors.

759. Stich, Judith, ed. *Financial Measures Conference: Progress in Measuring Financial Conditions of Colleges and Universities.* 1979. ERIC, ED 216 583.

Consists of a series of papers focusing on educational finance in higher education with applications to analyzing programs for the preparation of teachers.

760. Temple, C. M., and R. O. Riggs. "The Declining Suitability of the Formula Approach to Public Higher Education." *Peabody Journal of Education* 55 no. 4 (1978): 351-357.

Analyzes the use of the formula funding approach for public higher education and advocates that the system should be replaced with a more suitable system based on program outputs.

761. Tierney, Michael L. "Priority Setting and Resource Allocation." *New Directions for Institutional Research* 31 (1981): 29-41.

Describes the design of a resource allocation process that can stimulate faculty in teacher education programs to seek new opportunities for program advancement.

VI. FOLLOW-UP EVALUATION

762. Adams, Ronald D. "Follow-up Studies of Teacher Education Graduates." In *Advances in Teacher Education, Volume 3*, edited by Martin Haberman and Julie M. Backus, 181-201. Norwood, NJ: Ablex Publishing Company, 1987.

    Summarizes recent activities in conducting and utilizing follow-up studies of teacher education program graduates.

763. Adams, Ronald D. *Teacher Education Evaluation: The Western Kentucky Approach.* 1981. ERIC, ED 260 056.

    Describes the longitudinal follow-up model, Teacher Preparation Evaluation Program, developed at Western Kentucky University.

764. Adams, Ronald D., and James R. Craig. *National Survey of Evaluation Practices in Teacher Education.* 1981. ERIC, ED 260 054.

    Describes the results of a nationwide survey of the follow-up studies conducted by institutions with teacher preparation programs.

765. Adams, Ronald D., and James R. Craig. "A Status Report of Teacher Education Program Evaluation." *Journal of Teacher Education* 34 no. 2 (March/April 1983): 33-36.

    Results of a survey of preservice and follow-up evaluation practices at teacher education institutions are reported and interpreted.

766. Adams, Ronald D., and others. "Program Evaluation and Program Development in Teacher Education: A Response to Katz, *et al.* (1981)." *Journal of Teacher Education* 32 no. 5 (September/October 1981): 21-24.

Disagrees with the conclusions of Katz, et al. [*Journal of Teacher Education* 32 no. 2 (March/April 1981): 18-24] and reports that follow-up studies do make a difference in teacher education program evaluation and development. [See citation #814.]

767. Altschuld, James W., and Michael A. Lower. "Improving Mailed Questionnaires: Analysis of a 96 Percent Return Rate." *New Directions for Program Evaluation* 21 (March 1984): 5-18.

Describes the procedures used in a successful mailed evaluation questionnaire effort and provides guidance to those who are unfamiliar with the methodology of mail surveys.

768. Anderson, Laura, ed. *Following Up Graduates: A Measure of Academic Effectiveness.* 1977. ERIC, ED 140 684.

Outlines the use of alumni surveys to determine academic effectiveness of programs and provides suggestions for making the follow-up studies practical and useful for program improvement.

769. Ashley, Myra Gayle. "An Examination of Elementary Education Graduates' Expressed Opinions Regarding the Adequacy of Their Preparation in Teacher Education Programs in Selected State Universities in Alabama." Ph.D. dissertation, University of Alabama, 1976.

Presents a description of a follow-up study and its results that can be used in the improvement of programs for the preparation of elementary teachers.

770. Ayers, Jerry B. *A Fifteen Year Look at Beginning Teachers.* 1989. ERIC, ED 303 452.

Compares the first year graduates of the bachelor's level teacher preparation programs of Tennessee Technological University over the past 15 years.

771. Ayers, Jerry B. *A Longitudinal Study of Teachers.* 1980. ERIC, ED 189 146.

Describes the results of a longitudinal follow-up study of three groups of teachers who were followed for five years after they completed their initial teacher preparation program.

772. Ayers, Jerry B. *Study of the Teacher Preparation Programs of Tennessee Technological University. Report 86-2--Year XIII.* 1986. ERIC, ED 275 635.

Describes the results of the 13th year of the application of the Tennessee Technological University Teacher Evaluation Model and provides (1) copies of the instrument, (2) references to the appropriate ERIC documents for the results from the application of the model in years 1 through 12, and (3) a list of pertinent reports and other studies.

773. Bausell, Rufus Barker. "Teacher Training, Relevant Teaching Practice, and the Elicitation of Student Achievement." Ph.D. dissertation, University of Delaware, 1976.

Looks at the effects of teacher training and relevant teaching practice on the subsequent elicitation of student achievement.

774. Bellah, Charlotte Arant. "Preparation in the Critical Skills For Beginning Teachers: Comparing Perceptions Among First-Year Teachers, Student Teachers, and Supervisors." Ed.D. dissertation, Northern Arizona University, 1986.

Discusses the perceptions of student teachers, teachers, and supervisors of the teacher education programs at Northern Arizona University.

775. Benz, Carolyn R. *The Practical Value of What First-Year Teachers Have Been Taught in College: Implications for Teacher Competency Exams.* 1984. ERIC, ED 249 268.

Reports that, relative to certain competencies, expectations of new teachers may be unreasonable in relation to college preparation and events encountered in the first year of teaching.

776. Boser, Judith A. *Teacher Education Follow-up Surveys: Variables Related to Response Rate.* 1987. ERIC, ED 284 885.

Discusses a study to determine the relationship between graduate follow-up survey response rate and number of graduates, questionnaire length, and follow-up contacts and concludes that personalization of the questionnaire was one of the most important factors.

777. Brandt, Nancy Claire Schulze. "A Study of Relationships Between External Forces, Structure, and Organization and Innovativeness of Teacher Education Programs." Ph.D. dissertation, University of Nebraska-Lincoln, 1980.

Examines the extent to which various forces involved in change were utilized in two static and two innovative teacher education programs.

778. Brommer, Richard Allen. "A Descriptive Study of Graduate and Advisor Perceptions of Selected Components in the Unified, Non-Traditional Doctoral Program, Teachers College, The University of Nebraska." Ed.D. dissertation, University of Nebraska-Lincoln, 1979.

Identifies relationships that exist between graduates' perceptions of the doctoral program and the views and attitudes of the faculty advisors concerning these same elements.

779. Buffie, Edward G. *1981 Graduates of the Block Program. A Follow-up Study.* 1982. ERIC, ED 217 015.

Describes the results of a follow-up survey of students who participated in a Block Program of instruction at Indiana University in 1981.

780. Bull, Barry L. *Analysis of Data on First Teaching Certificate Completers at Five Public Institutions, 1982-83.* 1985. ERIC, ED 275 627.

Outlines the results of a follow-up study of graduates of teacher education programs in the State of Washington that was designed to determine the impact of program policies on the graduates.

781. Bush, William S., and Edward J. Davis. "Reflections on a Secondary Mathematics Teacher Education Program: Responses from a Survey." *Journal of Research and Development in Education* 15 no. 4 (Summer 1982): 53-62.

    Describes an undergraduate program for secondary school mathematics teachers, reports graduates' responses to a survey which asked them to rate the usefulness of courses in the program, and offers suggestions for mathematics teacher education programs.

782. Carter, Pamela, and Robert DiBella. *Follow-up of 1980-81 Graduates at The Ohio State University's College of Education Teacher Certification Program.* 1982. ERIC, ED 222 462.

    Describes the use of three different methodologies to conduct a follow-up study of the graduates from The Ohio State University's teacher education program.

783. Cheek, Martha Collins. *What Educators Reveal About Undergraduate and Graduate Experiences in Reading.* 1980. ERIC, ED 189 544.

    Outlines the results of a mail follow-up study that was conducted to determine the perceived quality of undergraduate and graduate programs in reading by former students in those programs.

784. Chizek, Jerry W., and W. Wade Miller. *A Follow-up and Analysis of Iowa State University Agricultural Education Curriculum Graduates: 1964-81.* 1984. ERIC, ED 246 741.

    Describes the results of a mail follow-up survey of the graduates of an agricultural education program for the period from 1964 through 1981.

785. Clark, Sheldon B., and James O. Nichols. *Increasing the Precision of Estimates in Follow-Up Surveys: A Case Study.* 1983. ERIC, ED 232 569.

    Examines the use of survey data concerning teacher education program graduates to demonstrate the advantages of a stratified random sampling approach, with follow-up, over a one-shot approach to an entire population.

786. Coker, Homer, and others. "How Valid are Expert Opinions about Effective Teaching?" *Phi Delta Kappan* 62 no. 2 (1980): 131-134.

     Discusses the problems in evaluating teachers using expert opinions of principals and other supervisors.

787. Comstock, Barbara G., and Joan T. Feeley. *A Follow-up Study of William Paterson College M. Ed. in Reading Program Graduates 1983-1987*. 1988. ERIC, ED 296 290.

     Reports the results of a survey of the graduates of the M.Ed. programs for the preparation of teachers of reading.

788. Craig, Robert, and Donald Freeman. *Survey of Advanced Degree Graduates of Michigan State University: 1982-1985 Academic Years*. 1986. ERIC, ED 280 844.

     Discusses the results of a follow-up survey of the graduates of Ed.S. or Ph.D. programs in education and provides comparisons of results with earlier surveys made of graduates.

789. Davis, Todd M., and J. F. Davis. "Telephone Surveys of Graduates Can Improve Professional Preparation Programs." *College Student Journal* 20 no. 4 (Winter 1986): 335-336.

     Outlines some techniques for conducting a telephone follow-up survey of graduates of a teacher education program.

790. Denton, Jon J. *Employment and Academic Characteristics of Former Undergraduate Education Students*. 1983. ERIC, ED 227 058.

     Outlines the characteristics of a group of graduates of the teacher education programs of Texas A & M University.

791. Denton, Jon J., and Michael J. Ash. *Graduate Program Evaluation Employing A Status Survey and Matrix Scores*. 1978. ERIC, ED 227 057.

     Describes a survey of former students from graduate programs in Educational Curriculum and Instruction and in Educational Psychology at Texas A & M University that was designed to determine graduates' employment patterns and professional profiles and their perceptions of the effectiveness of their programs.

792. Denton, John J., and others. *Perceptions of Former Students on Degree of Emphasis to Place on Pedagogical Topics.* 1985. ERIC, ED 261 997.

Reports that graduates in one study emphasize the pedagogical skills, classroom managment, instructional methods, legal and ethical aspects, measurement and evaluation, curriculum planning, organization and management of schools, and needs of special populations, in that order.

793. deVoss, Gary, and Robert DiBella. *Follow-up of 1978-80 Graduates at The Ohio State University's College of Education Teacher Certification Program.* 1981. ERIC, ED 217 030.

Reports the results of a follow-up survey of the 1979-80 graduates of the teacher certification programs of the College of Education at The Ohio State University.

794. Dilts, Harold E., and others. *Study of Teacher Education Graduates, Spring 1980. Academic Year 1980/81.* 1982. ERIC, ED 270 435.

Describes a follow-up study of the graduates of the teacher preparation programs at Iowa State University during 1980-81; document includes instrumentation.

795. Drummond, Robert J. *1976 Follow-up of 1970-76 College of Education Graduates, University of Maine, Orono.* 1976. ERIC, ED 141 306.

Reports the results of a follow-up study of the graduates (1970-76) from the College of Education at the University of Maine at Orono and includes instrumentation.

796. Drummond, Robert J. and others. *Teacher Education Internship Project.* 1986. ERIC, ED 272 475.

Describes the results of a follow-up study to determine the impact of the expansion and refinement of a clinical supervision model for undergraduate teacher education.

797. Duvall, Charles R., and others. *Follow-up Study of Indiana University at South Bend Graduates: Undergraduate and Graduate Degree Programs, 1970-83, Division of Education.* 1985. ERIC, ED 258 531.

Reports the results of a mail follow-up study of graduates' perceptions of the bachelor's and master's degree programs at Indiana University at South Bend.

798. Erdos, P. L. *Professional Mail Surveys.* Malabar, FL: Robert F. Krieger Publishing Co., 1983.

Outlines useful techniques that can be used for conducting follow-up mail surveys of teacher education program graduates.

799. Farrar, Carroll D. *Developing and Utilizing Undergraduate Program Objectives for Developing Evaluative Instruments.* 1980. ERIC, ED 206 729.

Describes the development of an instrument and a follow-up study of graduates of the College of Education at the University of New Orleans that is one part of an organized assessment program of the teacher education programs of the institution.

800. Felder, B. Dell, and others. *Reflections on the Evaluation of a Teacher Education Program: The University of Houston Experience.* 1981. ERIC, ED 200 519.

Recounts the experiences of the University of Houston in evaluating its teacher education program and in conducting follow-up studies of its graduates.

801. Fotiu, R., and others. *Undergraduate Follow-up Study: Spring, 1985.* 1986. ERIC, ED 280 842.

Reports a study of students at Michigan State University that begins when students are admitted to the institution and follows them for as many as six years after graduation.

802. Freeman, Donald J. *Compendium of Items for Follow-up Surveys of Teacher Education Programs.* 1988. ERIC, ED 298 097.

    Provides a list of items drawn from a wide range of teacher education follow-up and graduate survey instruments used by institutions from across the United States.

803. Freeman, Donald J., and W. E. Loadman. *Recommendations for Doctoral Guidance Committees Suggested by Follow-up Studies at Two Universities.* 1985. ERIC, ED 280 840.

    Analyzes follow-up studies of graduates of doctoral programs in education at two major state universities and reports that they considered alumni perceptions of doctoral guidance committee activities in planning course work, preparing and administering comprehensive evaluations, and guiding dissertation research.

804. Freeman, Donald J., and others. *Survey of M.S.U. Graduates of Five Student Teaching Programs: Trends and Long-Range Outcomes of Student Teaching Programs Suggested by a Survey of Michigan State University Graduates and Their Supervisors.* 1979. ERIC, ED 166 163.

    Describes a mail follow-up study of the graduates of five different student teaching programs and a survey of their supervisors to determine the effects of the programs.

805. Haney, Bernice Jedlicka. "A Study of Relationships Between Internal Processes and Innovativeness of Teacher Education Programs." Ph.D. dissertation, The University of Nebraska-Lincoln, 1980.

    Evaluates the processes involved in change of a static and innovative teacher education program.

806. Harrison, Jacquelyn. "A Descriptive Study of Selected Aspects of the Doctorate in Education at East Texas State University." Ed.D. dissertation, East Texas State University, 1976.

    Reviews the doctoral program in education at East Texas State University, reports the needs of its graduates, and suggests changes that should result in program improvement.

807. Hoffman, David E., and Susan Stavert Roper. *How Valuable is Teacher Training to Beginning Teachers? An Analysis of Graduate Feedback from a Rural Teacher Training Program.* 1985. ERIC, ED 258 967.

Outlines the use of a strategy for conducting teacher education program follow-up studies that focuses on the importance of the preservice program to the beginning teacher.

808. Hogan, Roseann R. "Response Bias in Student Follow-up: A Comparison of Low and High Return Surveys." *College and University* 61 no. 1 (Fall 1985): 17-25.

Reports a study in which the data set used permitted evaluation of assumptions regarding the effect of participation rates in student follow-up mail surveys based on such factors as demographics and relationships among the variables studied.

809. Holcomb, Zelda J., and William E. Loadman. *Supervisor's Evaluation of 1978-1979, 1980-1981 and 1981-1982 Graduates at The Ohio State University's College of Education Teacher Certification Program. Follow-up Project 1983.* 1983. ERIC, ED 248 204.

Describes a survey of student teacher supervisors for three periods and perceived strengths and weaknesses of the teacher preparation program of the institution.

810. Hord, Shirley M., and others. *Implications of Experience in Teacher Education Program Follow-up Studies for Future Work.* 1979. ERIC, ED 204 328.

Outlines an agenda of needed research and development work in teacher education program follow-up work.

811. Hummel, Thomas J., and Sharon M. Strom. "The Relationship Between Teaching Experience and Satisfaction with Teacher Preparation: A Summary of Three Surveys." *Journal of Teacher Education* 38 no. 5 (September/October 1987): 28-36.

Reports the results of three surveys of teacher education graduates and indicates that the amount of teaching experience may affect the responses given about the teacher preparation program.

812. Hyman, Marjorie Barrington. "Effective Preservice Experiences: An Evaluation of an Elementary Education Program." Ph.D. dissertation, University of South Carolina, 1987.

Reports the results of a follow-up survey of the graduates of an elementary education program in order to determine its appropriateness for the preparation of teachers.

813. Joels, Rosie Webb. *A Follow-up Study of Selected Graduates from the College of Education University of Central Florida: Final Report (#85-2)*. 1985. ERIC, ED 294 832.

Describes a mail follow-up study of the graduates of the College of Education at the University of Central Florida for the period 1980 to 1983.

814. Katz, Lilian, and others. "Follow-up Studies: Are They Worth the Trouble?" *Journal of Teacher Education* 32 no. 2 (March/April 1981): 18-24.

Describes a survey undertaken to assess the effectiveness of 26 follow-up studies of teacher education graduates which found the extent to which the studies' respondents were representative of the target population, types of recommendations resulting from the studies, and the extent to which information from the studies directed program planning and revision.

815. Keefe, Mark Wesley. "Returning to Teach: An Analysis and Profile of College Graduates Enrolled in a Post-Baccalaureate Teacher Education Program." Ed.D. dissertation, University of Massachusetts, 1986.

Analyzes the reasons that teachers return to higher education to pursue additional work at the graduate level.

816. Keller, David Lawrence. " A Follow-up Study of Secondary Education Graduates of the College of Education, University of Kentucky." Ed.D. dissertation, University of Kentucky, 1977.

Describes a follow-up study of the perceptions of education graduates regarding selected aspects of their teacher training experiences when analyzed by gender, grade point average, and subject area major.

817. Kelley, Charles Leo. "A Five Year Follow-up Study of the Professional Education Program of the College of Education at the University of Arkansas for the Years 1976-1980." Ed.D. dissertation, University of Arkansas, 1983.

Measures the effectiveness of the Teacher Education Program of the College of Education at the University of Arkansas for the years 1976 through 1980, as viewed by its graduates.

818. Kirk, Edward L. *Follow-up Studies of Teacher Education Program Graduates.* 1982. ERIC, ED 221 544.

Discusses the needs and values of conducting follow-up studies of graduates of teacher education programs, reports an analysis of ten reports submitted to the National Council for Accreditation of Teacher Education that reports evaluations, and makes suggestions for improving follow-up evaluation efforts.

819. Kirkeby, Michael Scott. "A Follow-up Study of the Doctor's Degree Graduates in the School of Education at the University of Montana." Ed.D. dissertation, University of Montana, 1975.

Describes the implementation and results of a follow-up study of doctoral graduates in education.

820. Koch, Norman E. *How'd We Do? A Follow-up Study of Elementary Teachers Receiving Basic Certification in 1986 from Western Oregon State College.* 1987. ERIC, ED 281 826.

Outlines the results of a follow-up survey of graduates of the elementary teacher preparation program at Western Oregon State College.

821. Larson, Richard Charles. "A Study to Determine if Opinions of Graduates Change with Teaching Experience Concerning Their Preservice Preparation Programs at Western Illinois University." Ed.D. dissertation, University of Northern Colorado, 1975.

Discusses the results of a follow-up study of the graduates of a teacher education program.

822. Leyser, Yona, and William Bursuck. "A Follow-up Study of Regular Education Students Trained in Mainstreaming Competencies. " *Teacher Education and Special Education* 9 no. 3 (Summer 1986): 136-144.

Outlines the results of a follow-up survey of 212 regular classroom teachers who took a course on mainstreaming and concluded the teacher felt that learning and physically disabled students were easiest and behaviorally disordered students were hardest to mainstream, and that the course provided a useful knowledge base on mainstreaming.

823. Lindsay, Michael. "Procedures for Follow-up Studies of Teacher Education Graduates." *Journal of Teacher Education* 36 no. 2 (March/April 1985): 29-33.

Offers systematic procedures for designing and conducting follow-up studies of teacher education graduates including recommendations for the formulation of questionnaires and scales to use in conducting the evaluations.

824. Loadman, William E. *Overview of the Student Information System Program Evaluation at The Ohio State University College of Education.* 1984. ERIC, ED 248 203.

Describes the Student Information System at The Ohio State University which has four main purposes including the documentation of student experiences for accountability and accreditation purposes, the diagnosis of student progress, the collection of data about students and programs for evaluation of graduates and programs, and the conduct of research on the nature of teacher education.

825. Loadman, William E., and Zelda J. Holcomb. *Follow-up of Autumn, 1978 through Autumn, 1982 Doctoral Graduates at The Ohio State University's College of Education.* 1984. ERIC, ED 248 205.

Describes the results of a follow-up study of the graduates of the doctoral programs of The Ohio State University from 1978 through 1982.

826. Loadman, William E., and Zelda J. Holcomb. *Follow-up of 1978-1979, 1980-1981, and 1981-1982 Graduates at The Ohio State University's College of Education.* 1983. ERIC, ED 248 206.

   Outlines a mail follow-up study of the graduates of the College of Education at The Ohio State University that was designed to collect information regarding job status, job satisfaction, student teaching experience, attitudes toward preservice academic training, educational background and aspirations, and demographics.

827. Louise, Carole. "A Follow-up Study of the Faculty Associate-Teacher Associate Program and the Traditional Program of Teacher Education at a Small Liberal Arts College." Ed.D. dissertation, University of Southern California, 1976.

   Comparison of two teacher preparation programs, the Faculty Associate-Teacher Associate Program and a traditional teacher preparation program, through a follow-up study.

828. Lyons, Carol A., and Marlin L. Languis. "Cognitive Science and Teacher Education." *Theory into Practice* 24 no. 2 (Spring 1985): 127-130.

   Describes the results of two follow-up studies of individuals who participated in a prototype cognitive neuroscience/learning style preservice teacher education program.

829. Martin, Oneida L. *A Score Plus One Year of Graduates' Perceptions of Their Teacher Education Program.* 1987. ERIC, ED 293 852.

   Summarizes the results of 21 years of follow-up studies conducted on 3,741 graduates of one teacher education program.

830. McKillip, Jack. "Applying Attitude Theories to the Return of Mailed Questionnaires." *New Directions for Program Evaluation* 21 (March 1984): 77-87.

   Provides a discussion of attitude theories as they relate to the response rate for mailed questionnaires and also discusses in detail such attitudes as behavioral intentions and involvement.

831. Melchiori, Gerlinda S. "Alumni Research: Methods and Applications." *New Directions in Institutional Research* 60 (1989): 1-98.

> Includes guidelines for setting up an alumni database and for conducting and analyzing alumni surveys that could be useful in teacher education program evaluation.

832. Mickelson, Marianne Vida. "A Follow-up Study of the Undergraduate Teacher Education Program at Drake University, 1980-1983." Ed.D. dissertation, Drake University, 1984.

> Analyzes data received from graduates of the teacher education program and determines their perceptions of the preparation program based on competency objectives.

833. Moore, Arnold J. *A Need for and the Role of Research Bureaus in Conducting Teacher Education Evaluations at Large Universities.* 1986. ERIC, ED 291 803.

> Describes the role and functions of a research bureau at a large university in conducting teacher education evaluations, in particular follow-up studies.

834. Moore, Kenneth D., and Sue J. Markham. "A Competency Model for the Evaluation of Teacher Education Program Graduates." *Teacher Educator* 19 no. 1 (Summer 1983): 20-31.

> Describes a system for assessing the level of competency of teacher education program graduates and using the information for program improvement.

835. Moore, Mary Helen. "A Descriptive Study of the Master of Arts in Education Degree Programs Through Continuing Education at George Washington University and Old Dominion University." Ed.D. dissertation, The George Washington University, 1983.

> Compares the perceptions of graduates of the Old Dominion University on-campus Master of Arts in Education degree program with the George Washington University Virginia Beach off-campus Master of Arts in Education degree program.

836. Nelson, Ann Marie. "Development and Field Test of a Teacher Education Program Follow-up Evaluation Plan." Ph.D. dissertation, Washington State University, 1982.

   Explores a plan for conducting follow-up evaluation of teacher education programs.

837. Ochsner, Robert. "Job-Related Aspects of the M.A. in TESOL Degree." *TESOL Quarterly* 14 no. 2 (June 1980): 199-207.

   Outlines the use of a questionnaire survey of graduates of the M.A. program in TESOL and reports that the graduates felt they were adequately prepared by their programs and that their jobs are satisfying.

838. Ogborne, Alan C., and others. "Dealing with Nonrespondents in a Mail Survey of Professionals: The Cost-Effectiveness of Two Alternatives." *Evaluation and the Health Professions* 9 no. 1 (March 1986): 121-128.

   Outlines the results of an experimental study involving health and social service professionals which found that a second mailing of a questionnaire to initial nonrespondents in a mail survey was more cost-effective as a means of increasing returns than attempts to conduct telephone interviews.

839. Pacheco-Molina, Manuel M. "The Merida Master's Degree Program in Education: A Follow-up Study Three Years After Graduation." Ph.D. dissertation, Michigan State University, 1985.

   Describes a study to determine opinions of graduates of the Merida Programs concerning the benefits to their professional development.

840. Page, Jane, and others. *Teacher Education Curricula: Perceptions of First-Year Teachers.* 1983. ERIC, ED 229 364.

   Reports the results of 300 first year teachers in a follow-up study which was designed to identify perceptions of undergraduate teacher education curricula, determine whether significant differences in perceptions exist among groups of first-year teachers categorized on the basis of background information, and determine which variables are most predictive of first-year teachers' decisions to continue as classroom teachers.

841. Peek, Patricia P. *A Successful Field-Based Program at Mercer University.* 1985. ERIC, ED 258 945.

Outlines the results of a follow-up study of graduates' perceptions and feelings about a field-based program in elementary teacher education.

842. Pegues, Wennette West. "An Assessment of Teacher Education Follow-up Evaluation in the United States: A Descriptive Analysis." Ed.D. dissertation, University of Tulsa, 1978.

Summarizes the state-of-the-art of follow-up evaluation in member institutions of the American Association of Colleges for Teacher Education.

843. Perry, Nancy Cummings. "Academic Qualification and Employability of Teacher Education Graduates." Ph.D. dissertation, North Texas State University, 1981.

Compares the graduates of one College of Education who are employed as teachers with those who are not employed, using the academic variables of grade point average, student teaching evaluation, and professional recommendations.

844. Pigge, Fred L. *An Analysis of the Responses of the 62 First Year Teachers Who Were Interviewed/Observed During Spring Quarter, 1981.* 1981. ERIC, ED 260 059.

Presents a summary of the responses of 62 first-year teachers to a follow-up survey designed to collect information and opinions about placement, experience, and intentions for further academic study; perceived need for and proficiency in selected competencies; where were the competencies developed; miscellaneous items dealing with majors, group, and professional requirements; off campus field experiences; academic career advising; and general reactions to the preparation program they had completed.

845. Pigge, Fred L. *Ancillary Findings of a Follow-up Study.* 1984.
     ERIC, ED 244 932.

     Outlines the use of the questionnaire "An Appraisal of My
     Preparation as a Teacher at Bowling Green State University" and
     discusses the findings of the completion of the instrument by over
     400 practicing teachers who were graduates of the institution.

846. Pigge, Fred L. *An Approach to Program/Product Evaluation in
     Teacher Education.* 1978. ERIC, ED 260 060.

     Describes the instruments and procedures of the graduate follow-
     ups and program and product evaluations conducted from 1970 to
     1978 by Bowling Green State University.

847. Pigge, Fred L. *An Appraisal of My Preparation as a Teacher at
     Bowling Green State University and A Programmatic Evaluation
     Follow-up of a Sample of the 1975-1980 Graduates of the Basic
     Programs.* 1983. ERIC, ED 261 979.

     Reports the use of "My Preparation as a Teacher at Bowling
     Green State University" as a follow-up device for gathering
     information for program improvement and development.

848. Pigge, Fred L. *A Follow-up of BGSU's Teacher Education
     Graduates of 1980-85: Their On-the-Job Performance and Their
     Evaluation of Elements of Their Teacher Education Programs.*
     1987. ERIC, ED 280 833.

     Discusses a follow-up evaluation of the graduates of the teacher
     education programs at Bowling Green State University for the
     period from 1980-85 in seven areas, including summary
     evaluations of the programs, evaluations of selected courses and
     experiences, teacher needs, evaluation of academic/career advising,
     comparison of job expectations and realities, concerns and attitudes,
     and suggestions for improving the program.

849. Pigge, Fred L. *Follow-up Evaluation Studies and Procedures,
     College of Education, Bowling Green State University.* 1984.
     ERIC, ED 240 083.

     Summarizes the follow-up evaluation studies of basic and
     advanced education graduates at BGSU with major emphasis on

determining teachers' perceived need for selected competencies that were part of their program of study.

850. Pigge, Fred L. *The Follow-up of a Sample of the 1976-80 Advanced Graduates. College of Education, Bowling Green State University.* 1982. ERIC, ED 261 027.

Reviews the periodic follow-up studies that are conducted of basic and advanced teacher education graduates at Bowling Green State University.

851. Pigge, Fred L., and Patricia L. Reed. "Teachers' Perceptions of Need and Sources of Proficiency." *Teacher Education Quarterly* 12 no. 3 (Summer 1985): 59-67.

Presents the findings of a follow-up study of 694 teacher education graduates' perceptions of need, proficiency, and source of proficiency; the implications of the results are also discussed.

852. Prine, Donald Lee. "A Follow-up Study of Drake University College of Education Graduates." Ed.D. dissertation, Drake University, 1975.

Describes the implementation and results of a follow-up study of graduates of education and their programs.

853. Raby, Elton Peter, Jr. "A Follow-up Study of Specialist's and Doctoral Graduates Receiving Degrees During the Years 1962-1975 in the Areas of Elementary and Secondary Education in the Department of Curriculum and Instruction at the University of Southern Mississippi." Ed.D. dissertation, University of Southern Mississippi, 1977.

Investigates the entrance variables and long term goals of the graduates of specialist's and doctoral programs and examines their opinions about and criticisms of their programs of study.

854. Robbins, Jerry H. *The Teacher Education Class of 1977 in Arkansas Institutions.* 1978. ERIC, ED 156 648.

Describes a follow-up study of the 1977 graduates of Arkansas institutions conducted to determine the graduates' current occupation: teaching in state, teaching outside of state, otherwise

employed, continuing formal study, military service, or
homemaking.

855. Rossetto, Celeste R., and Judith K. Grosenick. "Effects of
Collaborative Teacher Education: Follow-up of Graduates of a
Teacher Induction Program." *Journal of Teacher Education* 38 no.
2 (March/April 1987): 50-52.

Presents the results of a follow-up study of the graduates of the
Resident Teacher Program at the University of Oregon College of
Education in six areas including perceptions of participation
factors, training adequacy, benefits, current job satisfaction, and
future career plans.

856. Rush, Gary S. *Follow-up of Teacher Education Graduates 1983.
College of Education and Psychology, University of Southern
Mississippi.* 1983. ERIC, ED 260 062 (also see ED 260 061 for
a related study).

Reports the results of the annual follow-up study of teacher
education graduates from the University of Southern Mississippi,
that includes classroom observation of a sample of graduates,
completion of a questionnaire by each graduate, and ratings of
performance by supervisors.

857. Ryan, Kevin, and others. "'My Teacher Education Program?
Well . . .': First Year Teachers Reflect and React." *Peabody
Journal of Education* 56 no. 4 (July 1979): 267-271.

Outlines comments made by first year teachers that reflected on
their teacher education program and are useful in program design
and development.

858. Schmelter, Raymond Charles. *A Follow-up Study of the
Mathematics Education Majors from the University of Wisconsin-
Oshkosh 1960-1985.* 1985. ERIC, ED 265 034.

Explores the trend and apparent shortage of mathematics
teachers through a follow-up study of those individuals who had
completed certification programs in mathematics at the University
of Wisconsin-Oshkosh.

859. Schwartz, Henrietta, and others. "Curriculum Change: Implications for Teacher Education Pre-Service Programs." *Illinois School Research and Development* 17 no. 2 (Winter 1981): 19-24.

   Summarizes the results of a follow-up study that was conducted to determine the effectiveness of preservice programs in meeting teachers' needs for information about and the requirements of Public Law 94-142.

860. Sloan, Leroy V. *Morning Star Students: A Follow-up Study.* 1981. ERIC, ED 211 259.

   Describes findings of two follow-up studies of graduates of a Native American Education Center with particular emphasis on teachers in Native schools who are serving as role models for future citizens.

861. Stolworthy, Reed L. *Evaluation of Master of Education Graduate Degree Programs.* 1986. ERIC, ED 265 152.

   Describes a follow-up study of the adequacy of the preparation program provided by Washburn University's graduate programs as perceived by the graduates of the master's program.

862. Stolworthy, Reed L. *Teaching Competencies Demonstrated by Student Teachers and First Year Teachers: Tabular Illustrations and a Ranking of the Mean Values.* 1987. ERIC, ED 280 846.

   Reviews and discusses the results of two follow-up studies of the graduates of the teacher preparation programs of Washburn University for two years.

863. Stolworthy, Reed L. *Washburn University. Teacher Education Undergraduate Program Evaluation of First Year Teachers 1983-84.* 1984. ERIC, ED 262 010.

   Outlines a study of potential first year teachers designed to determine the adequacy of the preparation program they completed relative to the specific dimensions related to teaching as perceived by first year teachers, the adequacy of the preparation for specific teaching content and skills areas, strengths and weaknesses of the preparation program, and assessments of school principals regarding the first year teachers and their preparation.

864. Stolworthy, Reed L. *Washburn University. Evaluation of Graduate Programs 1983-84.* 1984. ERIC, ED 262 013.

     Outlines a follow-up study of the individuals who completed graduate programs at Washburn University, including copies of the instrument and sample letters to the graduates.

865. Sudman, Seymour. "Mail Surveys of Reluctant Professionals." *Evaluation Review* 9 no. 3 (June 1985): 349-360.

     Presents procedures for improving professional group cooperation in responding to mailed survey questionnaires including improving the cost-benefit ratio of cooperation, being sensitive to confidentiality concerns, and allowing respondents a full range of answers, including written comments.

866. Sudman, Seymour, and Norman Bradburn. "Improved Mailed Questionnaire Design." *New Directions for Program Evaluation* 21 (March 1984): 33-47.

     Identifies situations in which mailed questionnaires are most appropriate for follow-up and describes population variables, characteristics of questionnaires, and social desirability variables in depth.

867. Tabata, Yoshinoci. "Selected Factors Related to the Development of Graduate Programs in Teacher Education in Georgia Since 1951." Ed.D. dissertation, University of Georgia, 1982.

     Analyzes the relationships between trends in selected factors and the development of graduate teacher preparation programs in Georgia since 1951.

868. Taylor, Brenda Elaine Richey. "The Effects of an Early Childhood Education Program on Teacher Roles and Attitudes." Ph.D. dissertation, University of Michigan, 1979.

     Examines the differences in teacher attitudes and role preferences between those students who were early childhood majors and those who were elementary education majors.

869. Terrey, Elizabeth P. *A Study of Washington-Trained Education Graduates Pursuing Certification and Careers Out of State.* 1987. ERIC, ED 298 118.

Reports the results of a follow-up study of Washington State teacher education graduates during 1986-1987 who were moving to other states, seeking certification in other states, and obtaining out-of-state teaching positions.

870. Villeme, Melvin G. "The Relation of Teacher Attitude to Major, Employment Status, Teaching Level, and Satisfaction with Teaching for First-Year Teachers." *Humanist Educator* 19 no. 2 (December 1980): 85-90.

Reports the results of a follow-up study of teacher education graduates to determine the relationship between attitudes and these factors: employment status, sex, satisfaction with teaching, and long-range teaching plans.

871. Villeme, Melvin G., and Bruce W. Hall. "Higher Ability Education Graduates: Do They Enter and Stay in Teaching?" *Teacher Educator* 19 no. 3 (Winter 1983/1984): 11-15.

Reports the results of a study on education graduates in Florida which indicate that higher qualified graduates are entering and intending to remain in teaching positions.

872. Virunurm, Valdeko. "The Derivation of an Information Base For Academic Decision Making From Follow-up Studies of Recent Graduates." Ph.D. dissertation, University of Virginia, 1980.

Describes the derivation and utilization of an information data base for academic decision making that was developed from the results of a follow-up study of the graduates of a teacher education program.

873. Warren, Richard G. *Follow-up Study of Teacher Education Graduates. General Frequency Report.* 1982. ERIC, ED 270 436.

Describes one phase, follow-up evaluation, of a research effort which is part of the development and testing of a comprehensive teacher education evaluation model at the Iowa State University.

874. Whited, F. Moroney. *Survey of Graduates of Master of Science in Education: Reading Teacher Program, SUNY College at Brockport, Spring 1979.* 1979. ERIC, ED 182 683.

   Outlines a follow-up study of the Master of Science in Education graduates of a Reading Teacher Education program that was designed to help evaluate and improve the program.

875. Whorton, James E. "Special Education Teachers: Recruitment and Follow-up." *Teacher Education and Special Education* 3 no. 4 (Fall 1980): 29-32.

   Describes a follow-up study of employment of special education teachers, citing teacher education program admission criteria (specifically, nonacademic aspects) that may relate to employment.

876. Wiley, Gary James. "A Study of Selected Characteristics of Master's Degree Students in Education and Their Perceptions of Their Graduate Programs." Ph.D. dissertation, University of Southern Mississippi, 1980.

   Analyzes the relationship between 18 student characteristics and graduate students' perceptions of their programs.

877. Yarger, Gwen P., and Frank Broadbent. *Teacher as Change Agent.* 1982. ERIC, ED 217 013.

   Describes a follow-up study of teacher educators who participated in a special summer school program.

878. Yeaton, William H., and Lee Sechrest. "Assessing Factors Influencing Acceptance of No-Difference Research." *Evaluation Review* 11 no. 1 (February 1987): 131-142.

   Examines a study designed to assess the results of research that produce credibility when using mail surveys in follow-up evaluation work.

VII. INFORMATION UTILIZATION

879. Akpom, K. "Planning Program Evaluation to Meet Management Information Needs." *Evaluation Practice* 7 no. 4 (1986): 35-37.

Outlines some of the problems and needs in planning program evaluations that must be considered if evaluations are to meet the requirements of management for decision-making .

880. Alexander, Jay, and others. *Increasing the Use of Evaluation Information: An Evaluator-Manager Interaction Model.* 1980. ERIC, ED 185 040.

Describes an evaluator-manager interaction model that was developed to predict the impact of evaluation and research findings and also describes instruments for measuring the variables of interpersonal involvement.

881. Alkin, Marvin C., and R. H. Daillak. "A Study of Evaluation Utilization." *Educational Evaluation and Policy Analysis* 1 no. 4 (1979): 41-49.

Outlines the results of a study of the utilization of evaluation information for program improvement.

882. Alkin, Marvin C., and others. *Title I Evaluation and Factors Influencing Use.* 1982. ERIC, ED 219 444.

Explores the evaluation of Title I projects and indicates that the factors that contributed the most to the utilization of evaluation information were the reputation of the evaluator, the evaluator's commitment to evaluation use, the interest of decision makers, the extent to which the evaluation focused on local needs, the presentation of the evaluation information, and the development of

procedures that assisted decision makers in using evaluation
information.

883. Alkin, Marvin C., and others. *Using Evaluations: Does
     Evaluation Make a Difference?* Beverly Hills, CA: Sage
     Publications, 1979.

     Describes the use of evaluation results for the improvement of
     education programs.

884. Baker, Eva L. *Critical Validity Issues in the Methodology of
     Higher Education Assessment.* 1986. ERIC, ED 284 894.

     Discusses ways to improve the validity of assessment of
     college students and indicates that assessment should be used for its
     intended purpose, not just because information was available from
     a particular activity or project.

885. Barrios, Nina B., and Garrett R. Foster. *Utilization of Evaluation
     Information: A Case Study Approach Investigating Factors
     Related to Evaluation Utilization in a Large State Agency.* 1987.
     ERIC, ED 292 814.

     Reports a case study of the use of evaluation information in a
     large state agency which has application in the use of information
     for improving teacher education programs.

886. Boruch, Robert F. "The Administration of a Congressionally
     Mandated Study at Federal, State, and Local Levels of
     Government." *Studies in Educational Evaluation* 9 no. 1 (1983):
     89-104.

     Focuses on the administration of the Holtzman Project at
     Northwestern University, including constraints on its operation,
     the strategic decisions that seemed correct at the time, some
     decisions that now seem wrong, and the use of evaluation
     information in making decisions.

887. Braskamp, Larry A., and R. D. Brown. *Utilization of Evaluation
     Information.* San Francisco: Jossey-Bass, 1980.

     Outlines the use of evaluation information for the improvement
     of educational programs.

888. Brown, Charles I., ed. *The Role of Institutional Research in Institutional Governance.* 1980. ERIC, ED 208 774.

   Includes several papers related to utilization of information for the improvement of higher education programs.

889. Burry, James, and others. "Organizing Evaluations for Use as a Management Tool." *Studies in Educational Evaluation* 11 no. 2 (1985): 131-157.

   Indicates that evaluation can serve a variety of educational management needs if these needs are organized around a central concern, and if stakeholders use evaluation information so that their decision making resolves the central concern.

890. Collins, Elizabeth Carol. *The Impact of Evaluation on Community College Faculty Effort and Effectiveness.* 1986. ERIC, ED 280 529.

   Reports the results of a study to examine the relationship between college faculty's perceptions of the frequency of evaluation activities and their perceptions of their own effectiveness and effort in classroom teaching, curriculum development, professional development, college service, student advising, and maintenance activities.

891. Connor, Ross F., and others. "Measuring Need and Demands in Evaluation Research: Results of a National Survey of College and University Administrators about Desired Evaluation Services." *Evaluation Review* 9 no. 6 (December 1985): 717-734.

   Focuses on the distinction between needs assessment and demand assessment and presents a methodology for operationalizing and measuring demands and utilization of information.

892. Covert, Robert W. "Ways of Involving Clients in the Evaluation Process." *Evaluation Practice* 8 no. 4 (November 1987): 83-87.

   Outlines various ways of involving individuals in the process of conducting program evaluations.

893. Cox, Gary B. "Managerial Style: Implications for the Utilization of Program Evaluation Information." *Evaluation Quarterly* 1 no. 3 (1977): 499-508.

Characterizes managerial behavior in general, and draws some inferences as to how information utilization would proceed and how it might be increased in higher education.

894. Cross, K. Patricia. *Using Assessment to Improve Instruction.* 1986. ERIC, ED 284 896.

Outlines the use of assessment for the improvement of teacher education programs, emphasizing formative evaluation as opposed to summative evaluation or accountability.

895. Dawson, Judith A., and Joseph J. D'Amico. *Involving Program Staff in Evaluation Studies: A Strategy for Increasing Information Use and Enriching the Data Base.* 1984. ERIC, ED 244 979.

Reports that there was an acceleration of the use of evaluation information when the faculty and staff were involved in planning and carrying out studies.

896. Dawson, Judith A., and Joseph J. D'Amico. "Involving Program Staff in Evaluation Studies: A Strategy for Increasing Information Use and Enriching the Data Base." *Evaluation Review* 9 no. 2 (April 1985): 173-188.

Reports that utilization of information was increased through improved communication, staff perceptions of evaluation relevance and credibility, and staff commitment to the study.

897. Duckett, Willard R., ed. *Teacher Evaluation: Gathering and Using Data.* 1983. ERIC, ED 245 367.

Summarizes the results of a conference that focused on the utilization of information gathered from the evaluation of teacher education programs.

898. Fullan, Michael. *The Meaning of Educational Change.* New
York: Teachers College Press, 1982.

Summarizes the research literature on educational change and
describes how information is utilized and how change works in
practice.

899. Granville, Arthur C., and others. *The Impact of Evaluation:
Lessons Drawn from the Evaluations of Five Early Childhood
Education Programs.* 1978. ERIC, ED 166 212.

Describes five different program evaluations and indicates those
qualities which make an evaluation effective or not effective,
including how the evaluation information is utilized to effect
program change.

900. Gunn, Walter J. "Client Concerns and Strategies in Evaluation
Studies." *New Directions for Program Evaluation* 36 (Winter
1987): 9-18.

Outlines the role clients can play in directing, monitoring, and
promoting sound evaluation practice and translating the results into
policy.

901. Guskey, Thomas R. "Staff Development and the Process of
Teacher Change." *Educational Researcher* 15 no. 5 (1986): 5-12.

Presents a research-based model of teacher change which holds
that changes in practice and outcomes precede changes in beliefs
and attitudes of teachers.

902. Haenn, J. F. *Reasons Why Evaluations and Testing Don't Inform.*
1980. ERIC, ED 187 733.

Summarizes some of the major reasons that evaluations and the
results of tests are not used for program development and change
and offers suggestions for ensuring greater utilization of evaluation
and testing results.

903. Hall, Gene E., and others. *Measuring Stages of Concern About the Innovation: A Manual for Use of the SoC Questionnaire.* 1977. ERIC, ED 147 342.

   Offers a 35 item paper-pencil instrument for assessing individual concerns about an innovation and includes scoring and interpretation systems for the device.

904. Hall, Gene E., and Shirley M. Hord. *Change in Schools: Facilitating the Process.* Albany, NY: State University of New York Press, 1987.

   Presents a detailed description of the Concerns-Based Adoption Model, the procedures and instruments it offers, and includes recommendations for guiding a change effort in educational systems.

905. Heck, Susan. *A Procedure for Assessing the Implementation of Innovations with Possibilities and Problems. Research on Concerns Based Adoption.* 1983. ERIC, ED 226 455.

   Outlines procedures that can be used in assessing the impact of the implementation of innovations in a program.

906. Heck, Susan, and Marcia Goldstein. *Structured and Unstructured Approaches to Implementation: Whom Does the Shoe Fit?* 1982. ERIC, ED 206 107.

   Outlines both structured and unstructured approaches to the implementation of ideas and changes within an instructional program.

907. Hord, Shirley M., and others. *Taking Charge of Change.* Alexandria, VA: Association of Supervision and Curriculum Development, 1987.

   Provides a practical guide to organizing and guiding a change effort built around the Concerns-Based Adoption Model.

908. Huberman, A. Michael, and Matthew B. Miles. *Innovation Up Close: How School Improvement Works.* New York: Plenum Press, 1984.

Develops an explanation of educational change through a careful systematic analysis of case studies of change efforts.

909. Ishler, Peggy. *Upgrading Education Means Upgrading the Teacher Evaluation Systems: Merging Evaluation Information and Effective Teaching Research--An Inservice Approach.* 1984. ERIC, ED 241 486.

Outlines a project in which evaluation information was merged with effective teaching research to create a new atmosphere for administrators which utilizes information for program improvement.

910. King, Jean A. "Studying the Local Use of Evaluation: A Discussion of Theoretical Issues and an Empirical Study." *Studies in Educational Evaluation* 8 no. 2 (1982): 175-183.

Discusses evaluation utilization including examples where the rational use of evaluation results may be unclear or none existent.

911. King, Jean A., and Bruce Thompson. *Evaluation Utilization: An Annotated Bibliography.* 1981. ERIC, ED 204 363.

Includes a 23-item annotated bibliography organized around studies of evaluation utilization, practical discussion of evaluation utilization, and theoretical suggestions.

912. King, Jean A., and Bruce Thompson. *A Nationwide Survey of Administrators' Perceptions of Evaluation.* 1981. ERIC, ED 199 300.

Describes perceptions of evaluation held by principals, superintendents, and others who must use the information to make decisions.

913. King, Jean A., and others. *Evaluation Utilization: A Bibliography.* 1981. ERIC, ED 207 984.

Cites 326 references on the use of evaluation information, most of which were published after 1970.

914. Locatis, Craig N., and others. "Effects of Evaluation Information on Decisions." *Evaluation Review* 4 no. 6 (December 1980): 809-823.

Demonstrates that the amount of evaluation information given to a group prior to an activity will directly influence their decisions.

915. Madey, Doren L., and A. Jackson Stenner. *Policy Implications Analysis: A Methodological Advancement for Policy Research and Evaluation.* 1980. ERIC, ED 199 272.

Describes Policy Implication Analysis, which is designed to maximize the likelihood that an evaluation report will have an impact on decision-making, i.e., that the information will be used.

916. Mathis, William. "Evaluating: The Policy Implications." *CEDR Quarterly* 13 no. 2 (Summer 1980): 3-6, 22.

Lists ways in which evaluations may be biased, including policy or political purposes for evaluations, sources of policy or political bias, limitations and biases within the evaluation itself, and utilization of evaluation information in the policy process.

917. Meckel, Adrienne Maravich. "The Influence of Institutional Context on the Effectiveness of Follow-up Data in Promoting Program Change: The Stanford Teacher Education Program, 1979-1983." Ph.D. dissertation, Stanford University, 1987.

Examines the use of follow-up studies in the improvement and change of the Stanford University teacher education program.

918. Mowbray, Carol T. "Getting the System to Respond to Evaluation Findings." *New Directions for Program Evaluation* 39 (Fall 1988): 47-58.

   Provides suggestions for enhancing the use of evaluation studies for program design and improvement.

919. Newman, Diana L., and others. "Locus of Control as an Influence of School Evaluation Needs." *Evaluation Review* 10 no. 4 (August 1986): 536-552.

   Suggests, based on available research, that personal characteristics of decision makers influence how information is used in decision-making.

920. O'Reilly, Charles. *Evaluation Information and Decision Making in Organizations: Some Constraints on the Utilization of Evaluation Research.* 1980. ERIC, ED 205 600.

   Presents a simplified model of decision-making based on the utilization of evaluation information.

921. Ory, John C., and Larry A. Braskamp. *Faculty Perceptions of the Quality and Usefulness of Three Types of Evaluative Information.* 1980. ERIC, ED 199 296.

   Discusses faculty perceptions of the usefulness of evaluative information gathered through student ratings for improvement of instruction and makes suggestions for ways to improve information usage.

922. Paolucci-Whitcomb, Phyllis, and others. "Interactive Evaluations: Processes for Improving Special Education Leadership Training." *Remedial and Special Education* 8 no. 3 (May/June 1987): 52-61.

   Reports that teacher educators in the Instructional Leadership Program used interactive evaluation procedures (including numerical, process, and summative approaches) to inform their decisions about program improvement through a new training option for regular and special education leaders.

923. Patton, Michael Quinn. "Integrating Evaluation into a Program for Increased Utility and Cost-Effectiveness." *New Directions for Program Development* 39 (Fall 1988): 85-94.

   Outlines the integration of evaluation into a program in order to increase utility and increase cost-effectiveness.

924. Patton, Michael Quinn. *Sneetches, Zax and Empty Pants: Alternative Approaches to Evaluation.* 1984. ERIC, ED 242 068.

   Indicates that one of the major problems in evaluation is the utilization of information for decision-making and offers suggestions for improving the process, including utilization of relevant methods, active involvement of the individuals affected, having a clear focus to research, and clear action implications.

925. Patton, Michael Quinn. *Utilization-Focused Evaluation.* Newbury Park, CA: Sage Publications, 1986.

   Describes evaluation systems and models that are focused on providing highly useful information for program development and improvement and for making policy decisions.

926. Ripley, William K. "Medium of Presentation: Does It Make A Difference in the Reception of Evaluation Information?" *Education Evaluation and Policy Analysis* 7 no. 4 (Winter 1985): 417-425.

   Reports on the "how" or medium of presentation of the communication theory paradigm of "Who says what, how, to whom, with what effects?"

927. Roelfs, Pamela J. "Graduate Follow-up Surveys: Some Conditions Promoting Utilization in a Sample of Teacher Preparation Programs." Ed.D. dissertation, University of Arkansas, 1983.

   Examines patterns of program utilization of graduate follow-up findings.

928. Rogers, Joy J. "Using Evaluation in Controversial Settings: The Client's Perspective." *New Directions for Program Evaluation* 36 (Winter 1987): 33-40.

Describes how evaluation can bring time and an external perspective to educational policymakers concerned with making controversial decisions.

929. Rutman, Leonard, ed. *Evaluation Research Methods: A Basic Guide.* Beverly Hills, CA: Sage Publications, 1984.

Contains a series of essays on evaluation research with a particular focus on applications to program evaluation and utilization of the results for change and improvement.

930. Ryan, Alan G. *How Case Study Evaluations Are Received by Those Who Are Evaluated.* 1985. ERIC, ED 267 094.

Summarizes the results of a case study investigation to determine the best way to present the results of a research study such that they will be utilized for program improvement.

931. Smith, M. F. "Evaluation Utilization Revisited." *New Directions for Program Evaluation* 39 (Fall 1988): 7-20.

Indicates that if evaluation utilization is to be planned and measured, then the many dimensions of utilization must be understood by both evaluators and the staff involved in conducting an evaluation.

932. Stufflebeam, Daniel L. "Coping With the Point of Entry Problem in Evaluating Projects." *Studies in Educational Evaluation* 11 no. 2 (1985): 123-129.

Provides guidelines for choosing to do context, input, process, or product evaluation and summarizes some of the important points to consider in ensuring that evaluation information will be utilized.

933. Sybouts, Ward, and others. *A Systematic Approach to the Management of Program Development in Teacher Education.* 1981. ERIC, ED 200 574.

Reports a research study that was conducted in four schools of education to determine if there was any relationship between the degree of faculty involvement in program development and a systematic approach to change that involves a concern for the whole organizational structure rather than its constituent parts.

934. Thomas, Alice. *The Role of Assessment in Minnesota Institutions of Higher Education.* 1987. ERIC, ED 283 461.

Reports the views of chief academic officers at Minnesota colleges concerning assessment with emphasis on the use of evaluation information.

935. Thomas, Alice. *The Role of Assessment in the Private Institutions of Minnesota.* 1987. ERIC, ED 283 459.

Summarizes the results of a survey of academic deans concerning assessment and the utilization of information at their institutions.

936. Turner, Susan D., and others. "Fostering Utilization through Multiple Data Gathering Methods." *Studies in Educational Evaluation* 14 no. 1 (1988): 113-133.

Outlines means of fostering the utilization of educational evaluations for program improvement.

937. Turner, Susan D., and others. *Fostering Utilization through Multiple Data Gathering Methods.* 1986. ERIC, ED 269 453.

Presents a discussion of several factors which influence evaluation utilization and a case for the use of multiple data gathering methods as a factor in fostering the use of evaluation information.

938. Waugh, Russell F., and Keith F. Punch. "Teacher Receptivity to Systemwide Change in the Implementation Stage." *Review of Educational Research* 57 no. 3 (Fall 1987): 237-254.

Reviews studies related to the implementation of educational change and, in particular, focuses on teacher receptivity to those changes and to the utilization of information.

939. Weeks, Edward Clayton. "Factors Affecting the Utilization of Evaluation Findings in Administrative Decision-Making." Ph.D. dissertation, University of California Irvine, 1979.

Identifies the variables associated with successful information utilization, including organizational location of the evaluator, the decision-making context, and methodological practices used in the evaluation study.

940. Wholey, Joseph S. "Evaluability Assessment: Developing Program Theory." *New Directions for Program Evaluation* 33 (Spring 1987): 77-92.

Outlines the use of evaluability assessment as a diagnostic and prescriptive technique to determine the extent to which different problems inhibit program evaluation and subsequent use of the results.

941. Wilson, Steve. "Explorations of the Usefulness of Case Study Evaluations." *Evaluation Quarterly* 3 no. 3 (August 1979): 446-459.

Analyzes the claims made for and discusses some of the obstacles to using case studies.

AUTHOR INDEX

Abedor, A. J.; 655
Abrami, P. C.; 570-573
Abramson, M.; 1
ACRL; 684-687
Adams, C. R.; 133, 721,
Adams, R. D.; 133, 762-766
Adelman, C.; 252, 486-488
Akpom, K.; 879
Aksamit, D.; 168
Aleamoni, L. M.; 574-576
Alessia, M.; 279
Alexander, J.; 880
Alkin, M. C.; 881-883
Allbright, A. R.; 722
Altmann, H.; 280
Altschuld, J. W.; 767
Alvermann, D. E.; 453
American Association of Colleges for Teacher Education; 2, 3, 134, 169, 546
Amodeo, L. B.; 170
Anderson, B.; 171
Anderson, C. A.; 688
Anderson, L.; 768
Andreson, L. W.; 577

Andrews, J. W.; 489
Ansah, S. L.; 490
Antes, R. L.; 172
Antonelli, G. A.; 135, 558
Appingnani, G.; 547
Applegate, J. H.; 173, 281, 282
Armstrong, E. P.; 491
Arnold, D. S.; 136
Arreola, R. A.; 578
Arrozo, A. A.; 283
Arubayi, E. A.; 579
Ash, M. J.; 791
Ashburn, E. A.; 174
Ashley, M. G.; 769
Ashton, P.; 253
Association of Physical Plant Administrators of Universities and Colleges; 689
Astin, A. W.; 175, 492, 493
Atkinson, D. W.; 284
Augenstein, P. A. S.; 285
Austin, T. L.; 286
Ayala, F.; 493
Ayers, J. B.; 4-10, 62, 204, 494, 495, 770-772
Aylesworth, M.; 268

TITLE INDEX

Formative Evaluation Study of the Professional Phase of the
Pennsylvania State University's Secondary Education Program:
Study 1.0, A, 103
Formula Funding is Not the Problem in Teacher Education, 745
Fostering Utilization through Multiple Data Gathering Methods, 936
Fostering Utilization through Multiple Data Gathering Methods, 937

Generalizability of Student Ratings of Instruction, The, 571
Generalizability of Student Ratings of Instruction: Estimation of Teacher
and Course Components, The, 621
Generalizability of Teacher Behavior: Stability of Observational Data
Within and Across Facets of Classroom Environments, 456
Getting It Together 396
Getting the System to Respond to Evaluation Findings, 918
Goal-Setting as a Teaching and Evaluation Tool in Student Teaching,
440
Going Beyond the Data: Reconstructing Teacher Education, 569
Governance & Leadership in Teacher Education, 556
Governance of Reading Education: A Position Paper, 552
Governance of Teacher Education: A Struggle For Responsibility and
Control, The, 548
Graduate Education in Curriculum Planning: An Analysis, 96
Graduate Follow-up Surveys: Some Conditions Promoting Utilization
in a Sample of Teacher Preparation Programs, 927
Graduate Program Evaluation Employing a Status Survey and Matrix
Scores, 791
Guide for School Facility Appraisal, 700
Guide to Collection Evaluation Through Use and User Studies, 692
Guide to Coordinated and Cooperative Collection Development, A, 708
Guidebook for Shelf Inventory Procedures in Academic Libraries, A, 698
Guidelines for Extended Campus Library Services, 685
Guidelines for the Preparation of Elementary Teachers, 546

Handbook for Pre-Student Teaching Clinical Experiences. Secondary,
279
Handbook of Research on Teaching, 127
Helping Cooperating Teacher of Early Field Experiences, 299
Heuristic Value of Regarding Classroom Instruction as an Aesthetic
Medium, The, 383
High Costs and Doubtful Efficacy of Extended Teacher-Preparation
Programs: An Invitation to More Basic Reforms, The, 739
Higher Ability Education Graduates: Do They Enter and Stay in
Teaching?, 871

INDEX TO 1987 STANDARDS OF THE NATIONAL COUNCIL FOR ACCREDITATION OF TEACHER EDUCATION

STANDARDS:

I.   Knowledge Base for
        Professional
        Education, 8, 9, 29,
        40, 51, 53, 62, 70,
        81, 117, 124, 132,
        134-140, 142-146,
        148-150, 152-155,
        157-166

I.A.   Design of Curricula,
        8, 27, 29, 34, 53, 62,
        70, 151

I.B.   Delivery of Curricula,
        8, 27, 29, 34, 53, 62,
        70, 151

I.C.   Content of
        Curriculum--General
        Education, 8, 10-12,
        23, 29, 53, 62, 70,
        86, 96

I.D.   Content of
        Curriculum--
        Speciality Studies, 8,
        10-12, 23, 24, 29,
        53, 62, 70, 96, 151,
        156

I.E.   Content of the
        Curriculum--
        Professional Studies,
        3, 7, 8, 10-12, 23,
        24, 29, 53, 62, 70,
        86, 96, 101, 141,
        151, 156

II.   Relationship to the
        World of Practice, 8,
        9, 62, 79, 86, 87,
        124, 132, 202, 236,
        237, 248, 489, 495,
        519

II.A.   Clinical and Field-
        Base Experiences, 8,
        79, 87, 202, 236,
        237, 279-485, 519

II.B.   Relationships with
        Graduates, 8, 26, 86,
        87, 117, 202, 207-
        210, 219, 489, 762-
        878, 880, 881

II.C.   Relationships with
        Schools, 8, 54, 219,
        248, 489

III.   Students, 8, 9, 62,
        79, 86, 117, 124, 132

III.A. Student Admission,
        8, 62, 168-251, 501,
        515, 516, 520, 535,
        884

III.B. Monitoring Progress,
        8, 53, 62, 65, 183,
        207-210, 214, 241,
        252-278, 884, 894

III.C. Advisory Services, 8,
        53, 79, 183, 214,
        527, 674

III.D. Completion of
        Program, 8, 29, 33,
        37, 43, 45, 53, 54,

SUBJECT INDEX

Ability theory, 621
Academic ability, 175, 181, 217, 233, 260, 269, 534, 790
Academic achievement, 34, 59, 142, 156, 157, 190, 197, 198, 247, 253, 256, 258, 269, 275-278, 296, 300, 309, 323-325, 382, 469, 486-489, 496, 510, 521, 522, 542, 780, 871
Academic advising, 653, 825
Academic aptitude, 310, 527
Academic aspiration, 175, 826
Academic persistence, 488
Academic standards, 39, 110, 147, 178, 183, 187, 188, 196, 198, 199, 205, 217, 221, 226, 227, 229, 230, 249, 276, 369, 490, 514, 546, 548, 556, 567, 790
Academically gifted, 219
Access to education, 860
Accountability, 55, 90, 119, 128, 135, 166, 266, 325, 468, 486, 491, 626, 633, 758, 759, 934, 935
Accounting, 743, 751
Accreditation, 3, 9, 13, 15, 22, 24, 39, 56, 64, 72, 78, 94, 106-108, 111, 116, 119, 121, 138, 164, 169, 171, 221, 379, 477, 491, 556, 563, 759, 818

Accrediting agencies, 9, 15, 56, 106, 138, 491, 563, 933
Achievement gains, 325
Achievement levels, 267
Achievement ratings, 267
Achievement tests, 168, 182, 201, 234, 510, 517
Action research, 371
Adaptive testing, 262
Administrative organization, 49, 95, 114, 183, 553, 559, 561, 564, 566, 597, 617
Administrative policy, 224, 620
Administrative principles, 564
Administrative structure, 549
Administrator attitudes, 124, 390, 423, 569, 574, 629, 820, 845, 912, 930, 934, 935
Administrator characteristics, 893
Administrator evaluation, 5, 82, 227, 423, 517, 669
Administrator guides, 620, 733, 751
Administrator licensure, 81
Administrator opinions, 625
Administrator responsibility, 233
Administrator role, 729, 881
Administrators, 114, 315, 404, 553, 587, 669, 679, 891, 919, 923, 939
Admissions boards, 179